The Charisma Quotient

The Charisma Quotient

What It Is, How to Get It,

How to Use It

Ronald E. Riggio, Ph.D.

Dodd, Mead & Company

New York

First edition
1 2 3 4 5 6 7 8 9 10

Library of Congress Cataloging-in-Publication Data

Riggio, Ronald E.
    The charisma quotient.

    Bibliography: p. 205
    Includes index.
    1. Charisma (Personality trait) I. Title.
BF698.35.C45R54 1987   155.2'32   87-24547
ISBN 0-396-08962-3
ISBN 0-396-08963-1 (pbk.)

to my parents

Contents

III Charisma: How To Get It

Acknowledgments

FIRST AND FOREMOST, I would like to thank Howard Friedman for launching the research on charisma that provides some of the basis for this book. I would also like to thank the University of California, Riverside and California State University, Fullerton students who have worked as research assistants throughout the years (especially Barbara Throckmorton, Joan Tucker, Jan Hanna, Dale Hoy, Bryan Hallmark, Kathy Lang, and Laura Lindner). Thanks also go to several colleagues at CSUF and to Barbara Beckman at Dodd, Mead.

Much of my research reported in the book was supported by intramural grants from the California State University, Fullerton Foundation.

The greatest thanks go to Lila Samia, who has worked with me in developing the manuscript—from first word to last—editing, refining, and making invaluable suggestions. Thanks also, Lila, for living through the process with me.

The Charisma Quotient

✣ I ✣

Charisma: What It Is

❊ I ❊

Charisma: What is It?

John F. Kennedy, Franklin Delano Roosevelt, Golda Meir, Martin Luther King, Jr., Ronald Reagan . . . They all have something in common—they are powerful political figures whose decisions helped to change the world. They also have something else in common, something called charisma.

Politicians are not the only people possessing charisma. We see charismatic persons in films—the Robert Redfords, Meryl Streeps, and Dustin Hoffmans. There are charismatic religious leaders like Billy Graham, charismatic television personalities such as Johnny Carson, and charismatic sports figures like Muhammad Ali.

Most people think of charisma as a rare gift, something that a very few people possess. In fact, the term itself means a "divine gift of grace." But charisma is not something that is given to a person. It is not an inherited or inborn quality. Charisma is something that develops over time. More importantly, each and every one of us has the capacity to develop our own charisma. But before we can attempt to increase personal charisma, we need to understand more about it—what it is and how it is used.

Charisma is not a single characteristic or trait. It is actually a constellation of many different things. Charismatic people possess an array of important social skills. In fact, we have identified six basic social skills that, when combined, produce charisma potential. People who are truly charismatic use these social skills as powerful tools to make themselves attractive to others, to influence people, and to be liked and admired by others. Charismatic people are often successful in life—in their careers, marriages, and interpersonal relationships.

Although we typically think of charismatic persons as famous and unapproachable public figures, we each have encountered charismatic people in our everyday life. These persons enter our lives and often leave lasting impressions. One such person who was quite influential in my own was a neighbor named Damon.

Every kid on the block looked up to Damon. He was the neighborhood leader. Damon had a knack for organizing activities in a way that got everyone excited and involved. Even our parents trusted him. Moreover, good things always seemed to happen to Damon.

In high school, Damon was popular. He was student body president and voted "Most Likely to Succeed." Damon was not a particularly gifted athlete, yet he was an inspirational player—admired by his teammates and coaches alike. Throughout Damon's life, successes (and attractive women) have seemed to fall into his lap. But success has never gone to his head. Damon is always approachable, a friend to all.

I have only seen Damon a few times since high school. But each time I see him, I instantly feel comfortable. There is tremendous rapport. Even though our meetings are brief and infrequent, I always leave thinking how good it is to know Damon. I still admire him.

As I think back over our recent encounters, I can see now why Damon has had such a positive impact on me. He has charisma. It's there in his style of relating to others. Damon exudes a genuine warmth and caring, and he truly listens to what others have to say. He is an expressive and fascinating speaker. Damon is confident and self-assured in a way that makes others feel secure and at ease.

GENIUS VS. CHARISMA

In the early part of this century, psychologists began to measure general intelligence and developed the well-known Intelligence Quotient, or IQ test. Tests of general intelligence measure factual knowledge, mathematical problem-solving skills, comprehension of verbal meaning, and general memory. In the 1920s and 1930s, psychologist Edward Thorndike and colleagues[1] became interested in the type of intelligence that related to people's abilities to deal effectively with others and their knowledge of the rules governing social behavior. These researchers attempted to develop tests to measure these social skills—tests very much like those used to assess a person's IQ. But they ran into difficulties in measuring this "social intelligence" and in differentiating it from general intelligence. Soon, research on social intelligence was abandoned.[2]

Fortunately, improvements in measurement and in our understanding of human social behavior has led to a revival of this lost line of research. We are now able to measure social intelligence, and we are realizing how important it is for the development and maintenance of civilized society. It is social intelligence that allows us to communicate effectively, to develop healthy interpersonal relationships, and to band together for unified social action. It is social intelligence that underlies charisma.

We label individuals who have a great deal of general intelligence (those persons with the very high IQs) ``geniuses.'' We look to true geniuses, and their great storehouses of factual knowledge and problem-solving skills, with awe, admiration, and a little envy. In the same way, people gifted with extraordinary social intelligence, like Damon, who are brilliant and effective communicators, are said to have charisma. And we may also look up to, and admire, such truly charismatic persons.

People have had a hard time defining charisma. They are not always sure how to put charisma into words. But they do know it when they see it. People will generally agree on who is charismatic and who is not. In fact, the names of the charismatic individuals mentioned throughout this book were obtained by simply asking people to list charismatic persons; there is a great deal of agreement. It seems that charismatic people are easy to identify, but it has always been difficult to understand what it is that makes them charismatic.

Charisma is not something magical or mystical. It can be defined and measured. Our recent research focused on measuring charisma and trying to understand how it works. In the beginning, our intention was not to study charisma; rather our interest in charisma grew out of a series of research findings examining people's abilities to communicate.[3] We began to notice that individuals who possessed great amounts of communication skills were more effective in interpersonal relationships and in affecting the feelings of others. They also appeared to achieve greater and more varied successes in life than persons lacking these skills. As our work continued, we became convinced that we were on the road to capturing that elusive concept that people commonly refer to as charisma.

This book is about charisma. What it is. Who possesses it. How it is used to influence others. And how you can get more of it.

TAKE THIS TEST

Short SSI[4]

Read each statement carefully and then indicate how much the statement is like you. A "0" means that the statement is not at all like you. A "4" indicates that the statement is very much like you. Circle your responses. To find out your score, see page 193.

	not at all like me				very much like me
1. I have often been told that I have expressive eyes.	0	1	2	3	4
2. I often laugh out loud.	0	1	2	3	4
3. When I get depressed I tend to bring down those around me.	0	1	2	3	4

© Copyright, 1987 by Ronald E. Riggio, Ph.D.

	not at all like me			very much like me

4. I often show my feelings by hugging or touching others. 0 1 2 3 4

5. People immediately know when I am angry or upset with them. 0 1 2 3 4

6. At parties, I can instantly tell when someone is interested in me. 0 1 2 3 4

7. It is nearly impossible for people to hide their true feelings from me—I seem to always know. 0 1 2 3 4

8. I sometimes cry at sad movies. 0 1 2 3 4

9. People often tell me that I am a sensitive and understanding person. 0 1 2 3 4

10. When my friends are angry or upset they seek me out to help calm them down. 0 1 2 3 4

11. I am able to conceal my true feelings from just about anyone. 0 1 2 3 4

12. Even when friends try to make me smile or laugh, I am able to keep a "straight face." 0 1 2 3 4

13. When I am really not enjoying myself at some social function, I can still make myself look as if I am having a good time. 0 1 2 3 4

14. While I may be nervous on the inside, I am very good at not letting my nervousness show. 0 1 2 3 4

		not at all like me				very much like me
15.	I am easily able to make myself look happy one minute and sad the next.	0	1	2	3	4
16.	I always mingle at parties.	0	1	2	3	4
17.	When telling a story I usually do a lot of gesturing to help get the point across.	0	1	2	3	4
18.	I enjoy meeting new people.	0	1	2	3	4
19.	Quite often I tend to be "the life of the party."	0	1	2	3	4
20.	I could talk for hours on end on just about any subject.	0	1	2	3	4
21.	In certain situations I am concerned about whether I am doing or saying the right thing.	0	1	2	3	4
22.	While growing up, my parents were always stressing the importance of good manners.	0	1	2	3	4
23.	It is very important that other people like me.	0	1	2	3	4
24.	I often think about the impression that I am making on others.	0	1	2	3	4
25.	I am often concerned with what other people think about me.	0	1	2	3	4
26.	I can fit in with all types of people, young and old, rich and poor.	0	1	2	3	4
27.	I am usually very good at leading group discussions.	0	1	2	3	4

	not at all like me				very much like me
28. People from different backgrounds seem to feel comfortable around me.	0	1	2	3	4
29. I can very easily adjust to being in almost any social situation.	0	1	2	3	4
30. I am often chosen as spokesperson for a group.	0	1	2	3	4

❋ 2 ❋

Charisma and Nonverbal Communication

While on vacation several years ago, I was walking through a park in the center of a small town when something attracted my attention. Perched atop a white columned bandstand, a short, middle-aged man was making an impassioned speech. A crowd was quickly gathering, and I was also somehow drawn to him. The manner in which he spoke, his expansive and flowing use of gestures, the way he raised and lowered his voice, the tempo of his speech, were captivating. For more than forty minutes, his growing audience and I were held spellbound.

To this day, I have no idea what this man was speaking about. You see, I was in a small village in Mexico and he was speaking Spanish. Unfortunately, my knowledge of Spanish is limited to ordering *cervezas* in cafés. For nearly an hour, I had been fascinated, not with what this man had to say, but with the way he said it. This speaker clearly had charisma. What attracted me to him was not his skillful use of words, but his *nonverbal* behavior, particularly his ability to convey emotions.

A charismatic speaker should be able to use his or her skills to arouse and inspire others, to stir up the emotions in their hearts. But how is this done?

Words alone do not effectively convey emotions. If you ask a friend, "How are you?" and she replies, "Fine," you may immediately realize that her sad face, slumping shoulders, and slow gait indicate that she is anything but fine. Research has shown that when a person claims to be experiencing a particular emotion, for example verbally expressing happiness, but the person's nonverbal behavior is contradictory to that emotion (expressing the opposite or a different emotion), we tend to believe that the nonverbal behavior represents the way the person *truly* feels.[1] Effective communication of emotions usually takes place through nonverbal means.

However, nonverbal communication deals with more than just conveying emotions. Dominance (to show and to know who is in charge), feelings of self-confidence or anxiety, and liking for others are also expressed through nonverbal means. Yet, it is the charismatic individual's ability to effectively communicate in the realm of emotions that is one of the core components of charisma.

We communicate nonverbally through our facial expressions, gestures, body movements, and tone of voice. Our clothing, hairstyle, use of makeup, and the way that we touch others and physically distance ourselves from them also serve to communicate feelings and other messages. We all use these various nonverbal behaviors in everyday social interactions. What sets apart charismatic persons from others is their extraordinary skill in communication. Charismatic people tend to be eloquent speakers and effective listeners. They are skilled in the use of language—the verbal side of communication. But the truly charismatic individual is also a master of nonverbal communication.

EMOTIONS: A UNIVERSAL LANGUAGE

From infancy onward, we receive extensive training in verbal communication. Before a child utters his or her first word, parents have been encouraging the use of language. Great amounts of energy, and years of schooling, are invested in the development of oral and written communication skills. On the other hand, we receive little formal training in nonverbal communication. We learn nonverbal communication skills in a fairly haphazard, unstructured manner. Yet, nonverbal communication skills are critically important. As we have mentioned, they are a key element of charisma.

The words of the charismatic speaker I observed in Mexico had no effect on me since I did not understand the language. Yet, I could read the emotions in his face, voice, and mannerisms. The language of emotions is universally understood. It is one of the oldest and most basic means of human communication.

The roots of nonverbal communication, particularly the communication of emotions, are deep—reaching back in our evolutionary history. It was Charles Darwin who first began the systematic study of emotional communication. In his 1872 monograph, *The Expression of Emotions in Man and Animals*, Darwin speculates that ability to communicate emotions is inherited from our prehuman ancestors.[2] The communication of emotions, according to Darwin, played a critical role in our survival as a species and helped lead to our development as social beings.

One hundred years after Darwin, psychologist Paul Ekman traveled the globe to show that all human beings share the same basic emotions and express them in similar ways. Ekman traveled to a remote section of New Guinea, visiting a group of natives who had virtually no contact with the outside world. Ekman took along close-up photographs of the facial expressions of Americans who were trying to portray six basic emotions: happiness, anger, disgust, fear, surprise, and sadness. The natives were shown the set of photographs and then, through an interpreter, told a story that suggested a certain emotion. For example, the story designed to evoke the emotion of sadness concerned a man whose son had died. The emotion of disgust was brought to mind by a tale of walking through the forest and stumbling into a dead and rotting pig. The New Guineans were able to identify correctly the facial expressions associated with the stories. Ekman repeated these results in a number of different countries and cultures. His results indicate that these basic emotions, and the way that we nonverbally express them, is shared by all humans.[3]

EMOTIONAL EXPRESSIVITY: "THE SPICE OF SOCIAL LIFE"

The research that began our investigations of charisma involved examining people's abilities to express emotions. Although people everywhere experience the same basic emotions and display these through specific facial expressions, individuals vary greatly in the degree to which they are able to express these emotions spontaneously through their faces, gestures, and tone of voice. We all know people who possess a great deal of emotional expressivity. These expressive individuals make their emotional states readily known. They "color" their interactions with the expression of feelings. Emotionally expressive people are distinguished by distinctive and frequent changes in their facial expressions and variations in their tone of voice. Expressive persons are lively and animated. President Reagan and entertainer Ben Vereen are examples of such expressive persons.

On the other hand, we have all encountered persons who are not at all emotionally expressive. These stone-faced individuals are unable to display their emotional states spontaneously. Silent-film comedian Buster Keaton was noted for not giving outward indications of emotions in typically emotionally arousing situations. Ability to express emotions is a key ingredient of charisma, for it is through the expression of emotions that the charismatic person captures the attention and feelings of others.

MEASURING EMOTIONAL EXPRESSIVITY: THE ACT

Long before we began to think of studying something as elusive and difficult to define as charisma, our initial research team was concentrating on measuring emotional and nonverbal expressivity. We used two methods. One involved videotaping persons while they took part in a number of role-playing social encounters, for example, greeting a friend, describing a picture, giving a spontaneous speech, or attempting to portray different emotions on cue. These videotapes were then shown to judges, who rated each individual's expressivity using a variety of rating scales. Agreement among the judges indicated that this was a reasonable way to assess expressiveness.

We also developed a short, self-report scale called the Affective Communication Test, or ACT. The ACT is a thirteen-item questionnaire with statements designed to measure an individual's nonverbal and emotional expressiveness. Individuals who agree strongly with statements such as ''I can easily express emotion over the telephone''; ''I show that I like someone by hugging or touching that person''; and ''When I hear good dance music, I can hardly keep still,'' are likely to be expressive persons.[4] The ACT later became the basis for the development of the Social Skills Inventory, a more comprehensive measure, which will be discussed later.

Once we had determined who were our expressive individuals, we began to investigate various aspects of their lives. We soon realized that expressiveness is a powerful dimension related to social success. We found that college students scoring high on the ACT measure of expressiveness were more likely to have had experience in public speaking and were more likely to have held an elected political office in schools or clubs than were persons scoring low on the ACT. Expressive students were also more likely to be employed and to aspire to careers in areas that would allow them to have influence over others. For example, those scoring high on the ACT were more likely to have had sales experience than were students low in expressiveness. Moreover, these students were working toward future careers in counseling, public relations, and politics—professions that would require the possession of expressive social skills.

As we were examining these results, we ran across a story in a local newspaper about the number-one Toyota salesman in the country. This super-salesman had allegedly sold over 1,300 cars in a single year. We immediately mailed off an ACT scale for him to complete. The salesman's very high ACT score of 99 further suggested that expressiveness is an important factor in influencing others, and this later led us to believe that expressiveness is a key component of charisma.

CHARISMA AND EMOTIONAL CONTAGION

Charismatic individuals are able to draw others to them through their emotional expressiveness. An expressive person is an attention-getter. But can this emotion be transmitted to others? Can it affect them? Yes. Charisma, by its very nature, involves an ability to arouse emotions in the hearts of others. Through an emotional speech, a charismatic leader is able to "infect" followers, to stir them up to action. It is the charismatic speaker's skill in emotional expressivity that people most often associate with charisma. We have all witnessed this sort of charismatic power. A charismatic leader leaps to a platform, and through emotional pleas to the crowd is able to incite them collectively to action. An expressive football coach may go into the locker room at halftime, his team down by fourteen points, and through an emotional appeal, he is able to rouse the team. Newly charged, the team takes the field and marches to victory.

On the more day-to-day level, we all use our expressive skills to rouse others to action. We give a pep talk to co-workers or subordinates to try to get them to work harder. We try to rouse a tired spouse to get dressed and go out dancing. We use emotional appeals to try to influence others to donate money or time to our favorite charity. A knowledge of the emotional-contagion process can make some people, particularly charismatic persons, very effective at influencing others.

Years ago, we began to study the emotional contagion process and we were able to capture some of it in our laboratory. We were conducting a series of experiments in which students were paid to sit in front of a television and make judgments of videotaped facial expressions. The students would make these judgments in groups, and the sessions lasted about one and a half hours. The graduate students who were running the sessions began to notice something interesting. The emotional climate of the session seemed to be different for each group. Some groups were very interested in the judging task and remained alert throughout the entire session. Others exhibited signs of boredom, glancing at the clock and fidgeting in their seats. Some groups became irritated and a bit angry. By the end of the session, these group members would grab their pay and storm off, vowing never again to participate in a psychology experiment.

At first, we thought this was just random variation. But it seemed strange that the moods of each group's members tended to be in general agreement. Once we noticed this phenomenon, we decided to investigate the reasons for its occurrence. We began to pay greater attention to what was going on among the judges during the rating sessions. What we found was that the groups of students did not arrive at the sessions bored, bothered, or cooperative. Rather, the mood of the groups seemed to evolve over the course of the session.

Early on, we noticed that certain members of the group would begin to exhibit subtle cues of mood. A giggle, a sigh, drooping posture, fidgeting, or an alert head position began to help set the tone for the session, and the others began to be affected. Since each of the student judges had completed the ACT measure of non-verbal expressiveness before the judging took place, we took note of each of the student's scores at the end of the sessions. Those few key members, the ones who gave off the subtle cues of mood, were the highest scorers on the ACT! These nonverbally expressive persons—our emotional instigators—seemed to be influencing the moods of the other judges. We immediately set out to confirm this with a simple experiment.

New groups of students were administered the ACT. We then preselected three students from each group: one who was highly emotionally expressive based on the ACT score, and two who were unexpressive, low-ACT scorers. These three students were seated side-by-side in a small room and given a questionnaire that was designed to measure their moods. The mood questionnaire was collected and the desks were turned so that the three students faced one another. They were then given the following instructions by the experimenter: "We will begin the experiment shortly, but I'm running a bit behind and it will take me a few minutes to get the materials together. Please sit quietly and do not talk to one another. I will be right back."

The experimenter then stepped into the next room and closed the door. Exactly two minutes later, the experimenter returned and gave each subject a second mood questionnaire. Upon completion of the second mood scale, the experiment was over.

The analysis of the mood questionnaires indicated that the students arrived at the experiment with a variety of moods. Some were apprehensive, some a little bored or tired, and some felt content. Over the course of just a few minutes, there was a significant change in moods. The interesting result was that the low-expressive students' moods became more similar to the moods of the emotionally expressive persons. Regardless of the expressive person's initial or final mood, the two unexpressives' moods seemed to gravitate toward the mood of the expressive group member. For example, if the emotionally expressive person was anxious about the experiment (perhaps a bit wary of what these psychologists might be up to), the anxiety was transmitted nonverbally to the other two subjects and was reflected in more anxious ratings on their second mood questionnaires.

As we expected, and later confirmed, these expressive individuals were sending subtle, emotional cues through their facial expressions, body movements, and posture. In just two minutes, without uttering a single word, one individual, possessing this important expressive ability, was able to affect the moods of two anonymous strangers.[5]

The person who knows how to use emotional expressivity to arouse and incite others to action does have the power to influence others, yet people often allow themselves to be influenced. At times, we all feel a need to be emotionally aroused. It is what makes us feel alive. People seek out emotionally arousing forms of entertainment. We all enjoy seeing a good dramatic play or film, and the emotions that the actors convey may have an effect, making us feel concern for the character and, perhaps, bringing us to tears. Likewise, a good comedian should cause an audience to laugh, and, it is hoped, he will be able to cheer them up. But emotion-arousing entertainment is usually designed as a temporary escape from our actual emotional states. People may also search for a more lasting type of emotional charge—an attempt to find a more permanent change in their emotional outlook on life.

There are a number of individuals who make livings, in many cases very good livings, by giving so-called "motivational speeches." These motivational speakers are particularly popular with sales professionals, budding entrepreneurs, managers, and people who feel they need some guidance or life direction. If you watch these motivational speakers, they seem indeed to have an effect on their audiences. However, their actual ability to *motivate* the crowd may be questionable.

> A man in a navy blue, three-piece suit takes the stage. In front of him is a very receptive audience of over five hundred. In a vibrant voice, he begins: "This year my income is in the high six figures. Eight years ago, I owed more than $100,000 . . ."

> The speaker becomes an animated bundle of energy, striding back and forth across the stage.

> ". . . and I'm here to show you the way to a productive, financially successful and secure future!"

These speakers live and die by their abilities to inspire what is termed "motivation" (but what might more accurately be labeled positive emotions) in their audiences. In essence, they are able to turn their emotional expressiveness into a marketable commodity. While many of these individuals may possess a number of important social skills, and may, by our definition, be charismatic, their most important talent is the ability to spark an emotional reaction in listeners. Of course, it also helps if the content of their talk is entertaining, interesting, and easy to understand.

The process by which a motivational speaker "infects" the audience is the same process of emotional contagion we captured in our laboratory. More importantly, in a live performance, the listener is affected, not only by the emotional message of the speaker, but also by the subtle emotional cues given off by the surrounding audience members. As the speaker's presentation continues, the emotional reactions of audience members help to trigger emotional arousal in others, in a sort of chain reaction. The end result is that audience members leave feeling emotionally charged. Unfortunately, if the individual does not learn how to internalize the feelings of motivation—the emotional energy—the charge will quickly dissipate.[6]

While emotional expressivity is the key ingredient behind a public speaker's ability to arouse feelings in an audience it is also critical, in everyday social life, to our ability to establish emotional ties with others—to be able to show feelings of affection, caring, and concern. Inability to express emotions can lead to a lack of understanding between two parties and may eventually cause dissatisfaction with the relationship.

UNEXPRESSIVE PHYSICIANS AND UNHAPPY PATIENTS

Health professionals have been greatly concerned with certain costly problems that have been on the rise over the past several years. One such problem plaguing medical professionals is the increase in malpractice suits. Greater numbers of patients are suing doctors for supposedly inappropriate treatments, medical errors, and carelessness. This trend continues in spite of the tremendous advances in medical technology that have eradicated many once-common illnesses, increased survival rates, and improved patient comfort. Many physicians are being sued, not for neglecting the technical aspects of their profession, but for neglecting the personal aspects of medical care.

The stereotypical country doctor of the early part of the century had little to offer in the way of sophisticated medical treatments to cure the ills of his patients. What he did administer was a healthy dose of genuine concern and comforting reassurance. Today's highly technical, mass-production health care gives little attention to the quality of personal medical care—the "bedside manner" characteristic of the venerable family physician. Modern training of medical students emphasizes, almost exclusively, the *science* of medical practice. Little attention is given to communication skills and the *art* of medical care. It is not surprising then that patients try to rebel through increased complaints, court action, and even refusing to comply with their prescribed medical treatments.[7] A patient's dissatisfaction may thus be expressed in an attack on the physician (e.g., a lawsuit), or in refusal to follow the physician's instructions, which, ironically, only serves to hurt the patient.

In spite of the typically cold and impersonal world of modern medicine, there are still some physicians who are well-liked, trusted, and respected by their patients. What distinguishes these doctors from their unpopular colleagues?

A series of studies by health psychologist M. Robin DiMatteo and her colleagues indicate that nonverbally or emotionally expressive physicians are better liked by patients, and are in greater demand, than are nonexpressive physicians. More than likely, it is not expressiveness alone that distinguishes these doctors from those with a poor bedside manner. Physicians who are effective communicators are also likely to be sensitive to the feelings and concerns of their patients. They are sympathetic and able to provide comfort and reassurance.

Most surprisingly, there is evidence that physicians who are able to establish rapport with their patients are more likely to have patients who adhere to prescribed medical treatments. It seems likely that charismatic doctors, who are able to open up the emotional communication lines with patients, may not only have more satisfied patients, but healthier patients as well.

Emotional expressivity is an important part of charisma. It is perhaps the single most important ability. It is sometimes assumed that expressiveness—the ability to arouse emotions in others—is all there is to charisma. But there is more. Expressiveness is only the tip of the iceberg. It is the most visible component of charisma, the aspect of charisma that we can instantly recognize in our initial encounters with certain kinds of charismatic persons. But true charisma is deeper. Beneath the surface of the charismatic person lie other elements—skills that when combined comprise the powerful force of charisma.

EMOTIONAL SENSITIVITY: "I FEEL WHAT YOU FEEL"

A charismatic individual is able to give life to a speech or to social interaction by embellishing messages with emotions. Expressivity is one side of emotional communications. The other side is the ability to pick up on, or read, the emotional messages of others. Nonverbal sensitivity refers to an awareness of nonverbal behavior and the ability to decode nonverbal communication, particularly emotional communications.

Sensitivity to nonverbal and emotional messages is a second critical component of charisma. Typically, in the truly charismatic individual, emotional expressivity and emotional sensitivity go hand in hand. The good sender of emotional communication is also a good receiver of emotional messages. The rapport that a charismatic person is able to establish in a social encounter is built not just on the emotional transmissions of that charismatic individual, but also on his or her ability to read the subtle emotional messages emanating from the audience.

In order to understand more fully the role that these various emotional skills play in making up charisma, we have studied some famous charismatic figures. John F. Kennedy is the one historical figure who is most commonly mentioned as charismatic. Kennedy clearly possessed emotional expressivity, or as his biographer, Arthur Schlesinger Jr., described it, a "vitality."[8]

A young Nigerian diplomat also attested to Kennedy's nonverbal expressiveness:

> With Kennedy there were sparks . . . You meet him and "shoo-shoo," sparks and electricity would be shooting all over.

Kennedy was also extremely sensitive to the feelings of those with whom he interacted. He could establish rapport with his audience at a very deep, emotional level. Eleanor Roosevelt also noticed Kennedy's ability to communicate and the interplay of the President's expressive and sensitive emotional skills.

He had . . . total intentiveness . . . a superb listener
. . . he's with them completely . . . He would lean
forward, his eyes protruding slightly.

. . . his intelligence and courage elicit emotions from
his crowds which flow back to him and sustain and
strengthen him.[9]

These comments indicate that Kennedy possessed two
of the requisite six skills that make up charisma: emotional expressivity and emotional sensitivity. To be truly
charismatic, possession of high levels of all six basic
social skills is required. Of course, President Kennedy
and the other famous charismatic individuals mentioned
throughout this book appear to have well-developed skills
in all six areas.

MEASURING EMOTIONAL SENSITIVITY: PONS AND CARATS

Emotional sensitivity is an important social skill. It is
crucial to the development of good listening skills and
empathy. Of particular concern is the ability to read the
emotions of others. Effective counselors and interviewers
of all types tend to be high on emotional sensitivity, and
a great deal of research also indicates that good supervisors are those who are sensitive to the feelings of
subordinates.[10]

Two interesting techniques have been developed for
measuring emotional sensitivity. They are called PONS
and CARAT.

The PONS (Profile of Nonverbal Sensitivity) is a film
test consisting of many short segments of a woman acting

out emotional behaviors.[11] In some of the segments, only the actress's face is visible; in others, only her body; and some segments show both her face and body. There are also segments that present only voice tone without a picture, with the actress's words filtered out through a process called content filtering. The test taker is then provided with a choice of two emotional situations, such as fear and joy. The task is to try to determine which emotional situation the actress is portraying in each short segment. The total accuracy score on the test is the individual's emotional sensitivity profile.

The CARAT (Communication of Affect Receiving Ability Test) is a unique instrument in which the individual being tested (the receiver) views videotapes of spontaneous facial expressions. The persons in the videotapes (the viewers) are themselves viewing graphic scenes of either a sexual, pleasant, unpleasant, or unusual nature. The receiver's task is to try to determine which type of scene the person on the videotape is looking at simply by observing the facial reactions to the scene. The scenes are chosen to arouse reactions in the viewers. For example, the sexual scenes contain nudes. The unpleasant scenes are pictures of facial injuries and burns. After judging thirty-two of the natural expressions, the test taker is given a total score for sensitivity to spontaneously occurring emotional expressions.[12]

While both the PONS and CARAT are good tools for measuring sensitivity to nonverbal communication, other simpler measurement devices have been constructed. We have developed a self-report questionnaire called the Social Skills Inventory (SSI). You completed a short version of the SSI in the beginning chapter of this book. The total score on the SSI is your self-reported level of social skills—your charisma potential. Certain items on the SSI are designed to measure emotional sensitivity;

other items measure emotional expressivity. Still other items measure basic social skills that we will present later. But the combination of the basic skills measured by the SSI are the underlying components of charisma.

EMOTIONAL CONTROL: THE EMOTIONAL THERMOSTAT

The third component of charisma is called emotional control. While emotional expressiveness is important to charisma, we have all met emotionally bubbly, expressive persons who seem full of life and feeling. But as time goes on, they simply refuse (or are unable) to ``turn it off.'' They lack skill in regulating their emotional displays. For an individual to be charismatic, he or she must be able to control the outward display of inner emotions.

A close friend met a woman at a cocktail party and was immediately attracted to her.

> What I really love about her is that she's so positive. She's up all the time, and it's catching! When she's feeling good it comes right out. Same thing if she's feeling sexy. I keep thinking how great and fun life with her will be.

Just a few short weeks later, his passion for her had cooled considerably.

> It's like a roller coaster. If she's happy, great. But if she's mad at me, I've got to jump to get out of the way. The worst thing is that she can rub people the wrong way. If she doesn't like someone, she'll scowl at them—and when she's in a bad mood, everybody knows it.

Unlike my friend's ex-girlfriend, the charismatic person is able to regulate underlying feelings. Control over emotional communication is another important social skill.

There are times when it is important to stifle the expression of true feelings, particularly if they are inappropriate for a certain situation. The charismatic person is distinguished by an ability to hold back the expression of felt emotions and, perhaps, use a very different sort of expression to mask the true feelings. In other words, the charismatic person "puts on a happy face" even when feeling angry, sad, or anxious.

Throughout his life, the Reverend Martin Luther King, Jr., time and time again was forced to develop tremendous skill in emotional control. His nonviolent movement for social reform demanded it. During numerous unjust arrests, Dr. King was taunted and physically abused, but he kept his anger in check. When his home was bombed and his life and family were threatened, he was able to cover up his fears and anxieties and present a calm and temperate exterior. An eloquent and expressive orator, Martin Luther King was able, at times of great emotion, to put his own feelings on hold and present a peaceful or inspiring face to those around him.[13]

Researcher Mark Snyder was the first to try to measure this ability to control the expression of feelings. Snyder called this ability "self-monitoring."[14] Self-monitoring deals, in part, with the ability to fit in with the "emotional tone" of a social situation. An individual high in self-monitoring is easily able to blend in and become part of the crowd. If the situation is one where everybody is busting loose and having a good time, the person skilled in self-monitoring will let loose, too. If the situation is a somber and dignified discussion of world affairs, the self-monitor will also appear to be serious and concerned.

Self-monitoring is the ability to wear appropriate emotional masks.

The concept of self-monitoring was taken into account in our later attempts to try to measure emotional control. The ability to manipulate and control the expression of emotions is critical to skill in nonverbal communication.

It is true that nonverbal communication, particularly the ability to communicate emotions, plays an important role in determining who is charismatic and who is not. Yet, there is more. To be effective in influencing others, the charismatic person needs to be *socially* sophisticated and wise. While an individual possessing nonverbal communication skills may be able to touch others at the deep emotional level, the truly charismatic person also has skills in other areas, as we shall see.

❊ 3 ❊

Social skills and Charisma

While skill in nonverbal communication is important to charisma, charismatic persons are also distinguished by verbal skills and by their ability to understand the dynamics of civilized society and social life. The truly charismatic are not only socially sophisticated and wise, but they are able to carry on meaningful conversation and to adapt well to a wide variety of social situations.

A charismatic person's social intelligence in the "higher," more civilized aspects of social intercourse involves the possession of three additional basic communication skills. These three skills, which parallel our nonverbal/emotional communication skills, are *social expressivity*, *social sensitivity*, and *social control*.

The charismatic spiritual leader of India, Mahatma Gandhi, was known for his humble lifestyle, manner, and dress. Yet, he was keenly aware of societal rules and was adept at crossing both cultural and socioeconomic lines to converse intimately with foreign heads of state and poor villagers alike. Gandhi demonstrated his decision to develop his social skills when, as a very young man, he made a conscious effort to become an "English gentleman." He bought fashionable suits, changed his hairstyle, took elocution lessons, and became a party-goer.[1] As a foreigner easily recognized by his dark skin and accent, Gandhi realized the importance that proper appearance and conduct played in assisting an outsider to fit in with a particular social group or class of people. There is some disagreement concerning the success of Gandhi's attempt to fit in with English society. Moreover, as a young man, Gandhi was unable to speak in front of crowds. However, his methodical and disciplined attempts to overcome this weakness indicate that he was able to increase his social skills greatly, and thus, his charisma potential.

Although Gandhi's experimental venture into London high society was short-lived, the methods he used revealed the underlying social skills that would later serve him well in political life. It was Gandhi's well-developed social skills, and the confidence that he had in his communicative abilities, that allowed him, dressed only in a loincloth and sandals, to meet with Britain's ruling class, discuss crucial political issues, and capture the hearts of the common folk of India, Europe, and America.

SOCIAL EXPRESSIVITY: "SPEAK WELL AND YE SHALL BE HEARD"

Gandhi's charismatic power lay in his ability to speak simply and sincerely to those he encountered. As one of his followers later recalled:

> His tone was always conversational, even when he was addressing millions of people. Whatever he said was to the point, and he used mostly simple words to say simple things.[2]

Gandhi's charisma was distinguished by two factors. First, his addresses were simple and informal. This probably reflected his skill in targeting his primary audience—the uneducated lower classes of India. Secondly, Gandhi's tone was usually gentle. His talks did not contain the fiery passion usually associated with charismatic speakers. This, too, matched his goals. He was trying to arouse his followers in a movement of nonviolence—a calm, but determined, resolution. Jesus Christ and Martin Luther King were other charismatic leaders who used these same methods.

Gandhi's ability to engage different kinds of people in conversations on a wide variety of topics indicated his skill in social expressivity. Social expressivity consists of skill in speaking and the ability to initiate and carry on conversations. The socially expressive person is outgoing and appears to be approachable and friendly. Where emotional expressivity involves the spontaneous expression of feelings, social expressivity is related to the spontaneous translation of thoughts into words. Socially expressive individuals are usually able to speak automatically on just about any topic.

As you might expect, persons who are socially expressive have more friends and acquaintances than do people who lack this skill.³ It is important to bear in mind, however, that social expressivity alone is not necessarily the basis for forging a meaningful friendship. Possession of the emotional skills that we mentioned earlier are critical to the development of deep interpersonal relationships. But because the socially expressive individual is outgoing, he or she is likely to meet more people than would an individual who is unable to strike up conversations with strangers. Thus, socially expressive persons may develop a greater number of friendships simply because they have a large pool of acquaintances and a certain percentage of these naturally develop into closer associations.

My grandmother is a paragon of social expressivity. I never cease to be amazed at the number and variety of close friends that she has. The truly incredible fact is that many of these decades-long friendships were begun through chance encounters at bus stops, supermarkets, and while waiting in line. Of course, anyone who knows my grandmother has found out that she has not yet met a person with whom she could not start up a conversation.

Social expressivity is another of our basic skills that, when combined with the others, make up charisma. But too much social expressivity, without being balanced by the possession of some of the other basic skills, can have negative effects. High social expressivity contributes to a person who is a good ``talker''—a fluent speaker and who is able to dominate conversations. However, if the speaker lacks *emotional* expressivity, the conversation will seem dull and lifeless, even though the dialogue may be interesting and thought-provoking.

Recently, I went to hear a well-known psychologist-author give a speech. I was quite familiar with this author's published work and was looking forward to a stimulating presentation. When the speaker was introduced, he pulled out several typewritten sheets of paper, put on his glasses, and began to read the text of his speech in a low, monotonous voice. Try as I might, I simply could not keep my mind on what he was saying. After the speech, I asked some of the audience members what they had thought. They, too, had trouble following his lifeless presentation. A few days later, a colleague told me she had gotten hold of the speaker's typed speech and had read it. "It was really dynamite stuff," she said. "A lot of interesting and well-thought-out ideas."

The speaker did seem to have some verbal expressive skill, but since his speech lacked emotion (and dealt with some fairly complex concepts), it was difficult to follow in a face-to-face presentation. Social expressivity without nonverbal/emotional skills does not make a charismatic speaker. In the same vein, a person who is high on social expressivity may be a good talker, but he will not be viewed as socially skilled unless he is also a good listener and allows others to have their say in conversations. A balance of all of the basic social skills, including a balance of emotional skills and verbal/social skills, along with possession of skills in expressivity, sensitivity, and control, are all important to charisma potential.

SOCIAL SENSITIVITY: UNDERSTANDING SOCIAL RULES

. . . We must all learn the socially acceptable ways of living with others in no matter what society we move. Even in primitive societies there are such rules, some of them as complex and inexplicable as many of our own . . . I believe that knowledge of the rules of living in our society makes us more comfortable even though our particular circumstances may permit us to elide them somewhat.

—AMY VANDERBILT'S NEW COMPLETE BOOK OF ETIQUETTE

Throughout the history of modern civilization, guidebooks have been written, and courses have been taught, to instruct people in proper social behavior.[4] Parents begin teaching children the importance of good manners at a very early age. A thorough understanding of the rules that govern appropriate social behavior is the fifth critical component of charisma.

Social sensitivity is an awareness of the subtle rules that underly everyday social interactions. The socially sensitive individual is attentive to others and is a good watcher and listener.

Holden Caulfield, the character in J.D. Salinger's *The Catcher in the Rye*, illustrates many aspects of the skill of social sensitivity. Caulfield is a clever observer of people and their social behavior. Throughout the book, Caulfield demonstrates an uncanny ability to observe and interpret social phenomena that would elude a less sensitive observer.

Researchers Dane Archer and Robin Akert have developed a novel technique for measuring some aspects of social sensitivity.[5] The Social Interpretations Test (SIT) consists of a videotape of twenty different scenes. These scenes are from thirty to sixty seconds long and involve natural, unrehearsed social interactions. For example, in one scene a man and a woman are seated next to each other and are carrying on a conversation about their respective upcoming vacations. After viewing the scene, the test taker is presented with a seemingly simple multiple choice question: Are these two people:

a. Friends who have known each other for at least six months?
b. Acquaintances who have had several conversations?
c. Strangers who have never talked before?

Only persons gifted with social sensitivity are likely to notice the formality of the conversation and the lack of eye contact and realize that the correct answer is "c." The persons are indeed strangers.

Another scene involves three men who have just completed a winner-take-all poker game. Each of the men claims to be the winner. The confidence exuded by one of the men, and his simple and straightforward claims of victory, are clues that he is the actual winner. An individual who is correctly able to interpret all, or nearly all, of the twenty scenes would score high on the skill of social sensitivity.

Social sensitivity, as measured by the SIT, deals primarily with an ability to pick up on subtle cues in social interaction. However, our definition of social sensitivity, and the way that social sensitivity is measured using our Social Skills Inventory, is a bit broader. Social sensitivity also includes an awareness of appropriate social behavior in a given situation, and a concern over behaving appropriately in social situations. Social sensitivity is a very important, key component of charisma. It is a well-developed skill in social sensitivity that makes charismatic people appear to be extraordinarily clever, social "geniuses."

SOCIAL CONTROL: "ALL THE WORLD'S A STAGE"

Sociologist Erving Goffman, in his book, *The Presentation of Self in Everyday Life*, states that in our dealings with others we are something like actors in a stage play. We take on certain roles, and we wear appropriate "masks." We look to others for cues of how to behave or for cues that may foreshadow the course that the social stage play is taking.

Social control is skill at role playing, a type of social acting. The person possessing high levels of social control is able to play various social roles and is tactful and socially adept. He or she is able to adjust personal behavior to fit with what is considered appropriate for any given social situation.

Perhaps no charismatic figure was as masterful at the skill of social control as Eleanor Roosevelt. Whether she was playing the role of dutiful wife, White House hostess, political stand-in for her ill husband, or the role of politician in her own right, Eleanor Roosevelt was a skilled and impressive performer.

> Hers was always life with a purpose, and whether she spoke out as a wife, mother, daughter-in-law, or political onlooker, she had something to say.[6]

Eleanor Roosevelt's ability to fill social roles, in spite of her underlying insecurities or misgivings, further demonstrates this last basic component of charisma, called social control.

> She was a master politician—charming journalists, soldiers, legislators, housewives, farmers, and factory workers with her grace and capturing their imaginations with her vision of a better world. Beneath the surface of this public performance—always serene and orderly—was the private Eleanor Roosevelt, more vulnerable than the public figure.[7]

In part, it is skill in social control that contributes to the confidence exuded by charismatic persons. The awareness that one has the ability to perform well in just about any social situation—to fit in easily and comfortably with persons of varying backgrounds and interests—leads to the development of a type of self-confidence, or social self-esteem, in charismatic individuals.[8]

We were able to observe this relationship between social control and self-confidence in a study conducted a few years ago.[9] We recruited graduating college students who were about to take part in both on-campus and off-campus job interviews. We offered these students the opportunity to go through a practice, videotaped interview. The students would then be able to view the videotape and learn to correct any mistakes they might have made. Our interviewer was an experienced office manager who had interviewed and hired many job candidates and who would provide our student subjects with constructive feedback about their interview performance.

It should be mentioned that the typical job interview is a situation that calls forth the social acting skills of the applicant. The candidate for the job is attempting to portray the role of a competent and motivated worker. The interviewer's role is to try to see through any sort of social facade in an effort to try to uncover what the interviewee is *really* like—whether he or she will indeed be a good worker.

One week prior to our practice interviews, each student completed a long version of the Social Skills Inventory. In addition to measuring the three nonverbal skills (i.e., emotional expressivity, emotional sensitivity, and emotional control), the SSI also contains scales to measure the more verbal skills of social expressivity, social sensitivity, and social control.

An astonishing number of students signed up to participate in our interview study. Over one hundred students, usually dressed in business suits and with resumes in hand, arrived for the practice interviews. Immediately following the interview, the interviewer made detailed ratings of each student's performance. The videotape was also reviewed and the interviewer provided the student with feedback and tips on how to improve future interview performance.

We next assembled a panel of evaluators who viewed each of the videotaped interviews and rated students' performances, making an overall rating of how ``hireable'' each student was. Our panel consisted of individuals with hiring experience and a few trained student assistants. In addition, two personnel specialists viewed the videotaped interviews and noted significant errors and positive statements made by the interviewees—the things that they said that would either greatly hurt or help their chances of being hired for the job.

When we examined our various ratings of the interviews, we were confident that all of our evaluators were making reasonable assessments of the interviewees. Students who made many poor statements—statements that are taboo in a job interview, such as complaining about previous bosses, demonstrating a lack of knowledge or expertise in their chosen field, or poor grammar—were evaluated less favorably by our panel than were those who avoided such job-interview errors. Conversely, students who made very positive responses, for example, listing specific skills learned in previous volunteer or part-time jobs that would be relevent to future employment, were evaluated favorably by our judges.

Most importantly, as we expected, students who scored higher on the SSI social control scale were given more favorable evaluations by our panel of judges than were students who lacked skill in social control. Students who were skilled role-players appeared more confident and self-assured, and this behavior influenced the judges.

But the most surprising finding of all came when we examined the interviewer's ratings. She was overwhelmingly influenced not only by the amount of social control the interviewees possessed, but also by the six basic social-skill components—the charisma potential. She tended to rate the most socially skilled students as most employable, and, interestingly, she seemed to miss many of the errors committed by these charismatic interviewees. Our interviewer was, in a sense, duped by the socially skilled students. (To be fair to the interviewer, this was not so much her fault as it was related to the skills of the interviewees.) The charismatic students were able to engage her attention in such a way that it was difficult for her to step back and critically evaluate what they were actually saying. She was charmed by their smooth, skilled performance in the job interview. On the other hand, our panel of evaluators were watching the video-taped interviews from a third-party perspective. Although they, too, responded favorably to the charismatic interviewees' socially skilled performance, they were less affected. The explanation is that the evaluators were more removed from the charismatic interviewees' performances. They were less likely to be captivated by the charismatic interviewees' social skills since the interviewees were directing their performance to the interviewer, not to the camera. This is somewhat akin to the motivational speaker who is much more effective in a face-to-face, rather than recorded, performance.

Some of the results that we found in our job-interview study have been replicated a number of times.[10] In general, they show that charismatic persons are more effective in influencing others in direct, face-to-face encounters where the full impact of their powerful and highly refined social skills are aimed squarely at the target persons.

SOCIAL SKILLS
AND DECEPTION

There is, perhaps, no social ability that is more complex, or more human, than the ability to deceive.[11] Deception and attempts at deception have become a common, integral part of everyday social life. Deception may involve malicious and self-serving lies, such as a worker who provides a supervisor with false and damaging information about a co-worker in order to enhance his own chances for a promotion. Deception may also involve the little "white lies" that we might tell a spouse or a lover to cover up some minor transgression. In contrast, certain lies may have the intention of protecting another's feelings, such as telling a friend that her appalling new hairstyle is very becoming.

While lies take many forms, they usually involve one of two types of strategies. People try to lie by being convincing—by relating a plausible story in a straightforward, honest manner. The second general deception strategy usually involves covering up true feelings by either presenting a calm, guilt-free exterior, or, in certain instances, using a conflicting emotional state as a mask.

Regardless of the type of lie, success at deception should be directly related to possession of basic social skills. Skills in social expressivity and social control are critical to telling plausible lies. The skill of emotional control is the key behind covering up feelings, especially feelings of guilt. Charismatic persons, then, should be more successful than nonsocially skilled persons at deceiving.

In his recent book, *Telling Lies*, psychologist Paul Ekman outlines two celebrated instances of deception, both of which were committed by persons who have been characterized as charismatic.

The first lie was perpetrated by Adolf Hitler, whose deception involved giving a plausible verbal performance.

In 1938, Hitler's armies were moving into place for an invasion of Czechoslovakia. Trying to buy a little more time to prepare the attack, Hitler met with the prime minister of Great Britain, Neville Chamberlain. Keeping his true plans concealed, and with a cover story of trying to maintain peace, Hitler was able to convince Chamberlain to persuade the Czechs not to mobilize their army. Hitler's deception was soon revealed when he quickly overran Czechoslovakia.

Twenty-four years later, the second famous instance of deception took place.

In the early days of the Cuban missile crisis, John F. Kennedy met with Soviet Foreign Minister Andrei Gromyko. Two days earlier, Kennedy had discovered conclusive evidence that the Soviets, despite denials, had placed offensive missiles in Cuba.

President Kennedy's deception involved withholding his knowledge of the missiles. He did not want to "let on" to Gromyko that he had irrefutable evidence of their existence. During their meeting, Gromyko continued the Soviet cover story that the missiles in Cuba were actually anti-aircraft guns. Obviously, Gromyko was unaware that Kennedy knew the truth. Despite his underlying anger at the Soviet's deception, Kennedy remained calm throughout the meeting, withholding his true knowledge and feelings.

What skills were most likely being used by Hitler and Kennedy to assist in their successful deceits? In all probability, Hitler's skill in social control was of the utmost importance to him. As Ekman points out, Hitler was a practiced and capable deceiver.

> He could turn on charm or fury and could with great mastery impress or intimidate, inhibit, or falsify feelings and plans.[12]

Hitler was, in effect, playing a role that he felt critical in achieving his desired political and military goals. He was coolly detached from emotions in this particular situation. Kennedy, on the other hand, was exercising emotional control. The success of his deception depended on his ability to keep his true feelings in check.

In short, different types of lies may call for different types of basic social skills. However, the charismatic person has an advantage, for he or she possesses a wide and balanced range of these basic social skills and is able to summon them as needed.

In a series of studies, we examined in great detail the role that basic social skills and charisma play in the ability to deceive others successfully. In these studies, we used two different kinds of deception. The first involved making up inaccurate responses to questions about pictures. Volunteers were videotaped as they described pictures that they had just viewed. Below each picture was an instruction either to describe the picture truthfully or falsely. We then showed these videotaped descriptions to groups of judges, who attempted to determine if each segment was a lie or the truth.

Our second type of deception involved videotaping students giving short, persuasive speeches advocating certain positions on controversial topics (e.g., legalized abortion, capital punishment). However, two weeks before the students took part in the experiment, we had measured their attitudes on each of the controversial topics as part of a class exercise. We used this information to preselect the topics on which they were to speak. Topics were chosen so that sometimes subjects would give speeches advocating a position that they actually believed. This constituted our truth-telling condition. For the other speeches, they were instructed to argue for a position that was directly opposed to their actual attitude about the subject. These were the deceptions. The videotaped speeches were then shown to judges, whose task was to determine whether the students actually believed or did not believe what they were saying. We also obtained measures of the basic social skills of the subjects in each of the experiments.[13]

The results indicated that individuals who scored high on scales of social control were better deceivers, particularly in our second deception task where they were, in effect, playing the role of a "pitchman" trying to sell others on a particular point of view. To a lesser extent, persons who scored high on measures of emotional control and social expressivity also tended to be better liars. However, when we examined these results more closely, we realized that much of their deception skill was related to the fact that these socially skilled subjects were simply seen as more truthful in all cases—regardless of whether they were lying or telling the truth. Judges just seemed to believe certain people more than others. We realized that those persons with high charisma potential, particularly those possessing expressive and controlling skills, had what we called an ''honest demeanor.'' They simply looked more honest than non-socially skilled persons.

Our next step was to try to determine what it is that charismatic people do that makes them appear to be more honest. To do this, we painstakingly analyzed the nonverbal and verbal behaviors that each individual displayed each time he lied or told the truth. We found that socially skilled individuals tended to speak faster and more fluently than did nonskilled persons. The socially skilled deceivers also tended to display fewer stereotypically ''nervous'' nonverbal cues such as shifting in their seats, or rubbing or scratching themselves. All of these cues tended to impress our judges favorably, who rated the socially skilled individuals as more honest overall.

SEX DIFFERENCES IN SOCIAL SKILLS

Are men or women more likely to be charismatic? Our evidence seems to indicate that females may have a slight edge, particularly in the area of nonverbal and emotional skills. Women tend to have more charisma potential than men, based on their total possession of basic social skills. This may seem somewhat surprising, particularly when you consider that most of the charismatic leaders and public figures that immediately come to mind are males. However, the latter difference may be due more to our male-dominated political systems rather than to any actual charisma differences in men and women.

Years of research have found that women are much better emotional communicators than are men.[14] Women are simply better able to express feelings. This may have a great deal to do with the way we raise our children. Traditionally, when a little girl is injured she cries, runs to her mother or father, and receives comfort and reassurance. In the same circumstances, a young boy might be encouraged to stop crying and ''take it like a man.'' Of course, these traditional child-rearing practices are changing, but differences in the treatment of the sexes still exist and probably account for many important communication and social-skill differences in women and men. The net result is that women develop their expressive skills while men are taught to control expression.

We often hear the term ''women's intuition.'' It refers to an apparent special sense that women have—an ability to know what is going on even before words are spoken or actions are taken. Is intuition some psychic power or sixth sense? Probably not. It seems that intuition actually reflects a sex difference in basic social skills. Women are more emotionally and socially sensitive than men. In general, women are better able to read both the nonverbal and social cues emanating from others. Since many of these cues are very subtle, perhaps detectable at an almost subconscious level (and perhaps eluding many men altogether), we may incorrectly infer that sensitivity is some sort of psychic of telepathic power. Many stage ''psychics'' finely hone their abilities to read subtle cues in others' behavior to such an extent that they seem to know information about people that could have only been obtained through mystical or supernatural powers.

In summary, women are generally more emotionally and verbally expressive than men. They are also more sensitive to the emotional communications of others and to understanding and interpreting social rules (i.e., social sensitivity). This makes sense since women, as a group, are socialized to be more aware of, and concerned for, the feelings of others, than are men.

Men, on the other hand, are more skilled at emotional control and may be slightly better than women at certain role-playing and manipulative skills.[15] Again, this is probably due more to men receiving greater practice in controlling their emotional and verbal expressions than to any inherent differences in the communication potential of men and women. Of course, we are talking in generalities. These social-skill disparities represent differences in men and women as a whole and do not preclude the fact that there are men who are very skilled in emotional expressivity and sensitivity, or that there are women who are masters of emotional control.

Moreover, traditional sex roles are changing, and the distinctions between male and female roles are becoming less and less obvious. In the same way, political and societal rules that have discriminated against women—making it difficult for charismatic women to achieve positions of power and influence—are changing. As we learn to accept the importance of effective communication at both the social and the emotional levels, and as we develop our communication potentials, distinctions between men and women in this area are likely to disappear.

SOCIAL SKILLS AND CHARISMA: PUTTING IT ALL TOGETHER

Earlier, we mentioned that charisma is not a single characteristic, but a composite of six basic social skills. The SSI test in Chapter 1 measured the six basic social skills and added them to obtain a total score for charisma potential. While this is a useful and generally accurate way to measure potential charisma, there are also some dangers. The simple amount of each basic skill is, of course, an important contributor to charisma. The basic social skills are added together to determine charisma potential. But the skills must also be in balance. If any of the basic skill levels is disproportionately high or low in relation to the other basic skills, it may lead to problems and an actual reduction of charisma potential. For example, too much sensitivity, without expressive and control skills, can lead to social anxiety and perhaps, in extreme, to withdrawal from social life. Similarly, a person extremely high on social control, but lacking other important basic skills, may become a "social chameleon"—able to adapt to just about any social situation, but unable to express his or her own feelings and perhaps unable to establish meaningful ties with others.

When I first began to suggest that charisma was actually a composite of well-developed, basic social skills—a type of advanced social intelligence—one of my graduate research assistants was skeptical. She agreed with our research findings that social skills contributed to success in social interaction and ability to influence people, but she disagreed with my assertion that social skills equalled charisma.

"Charisma is something more. It's hard to define," she said. "But it's a quality you *feel*."

How could we test my hypothesis in a way that would convince her? We already knew that people generally agree on famous persons who are or were charismatic. But those were well-known public figures. What about charisma in the general population? I challenged the student to go out and find charismatic persons in the community and test their social skills. She came up with a very straightforward way of doing this. She recruited eighteen volunteers from a college class. Each of these class members was given two copies of the long version of the Social Skills Inventory. The volunteers were instructed to give one copy to the *most* charismatic person they knew and to give the second copy to the *least* charismatic person they could find. The volunteers were also asked to use a nine-point scale to rate how charismatic or noncharismatic their two acquaintances were. This was done as a check in case certain volunteers did not feel that the two persons differed greatly on charisma.

As expected, the persons who our volunteers considered charismatic scored about fifty points higher on the Social Skills Inventory than did the persons whom they had labeled noncharismatic. This difference was especially significant since our volunteers had difficulty finding extremely charismatic and noncharismatic persons. By the volunteers' ratings, the average difference between charismatics and noncharismatics was only about four points on the nine-point scale.[16]

In a second series of studies designed to confirm that possession of social skills equals possession of charisma potential, we used our videotaped samples of people's behavior obtained in our experiments. These videotapes consisted of research subjects who had completed the SSI and who had been videotaped in a variety of different social interactions (e.g., being interviewed, meeting new people). We had groups view these short samples of the subjects' behavior and independently rate how charismatic each person appeared to be. There was remarkable agreement among the judges. The raters generally agreed on who was charismatic and who was not. Total scores on the SSI were also strongly related to how charismatic the subjects appeared. The more socially skilled the person was, the more charismatic he or she appeared to others.

The six basic social skills we have been discussing represent a charisma *potential*. Possessing these skills in great amounts, and in balance, means that socially skilled persons have an aptitude for influencing others. Typically, as social skills develop, an individual also learns specific strategies of influence. The person learns that there are certain regularities to human behavior, that people tend to follow definite social rules. Knowing how these rules operate and how to manipulate them can be the key to unlocking charisma potential and using it to affect others. We will learn more about how charisma is used to influence others in Part II of this book. But before that, we need to examine the role that social skills play in making the charismatic person attractive to others.

✳ 4 ✳

Charisma and Physical Attractiveness

"See the new, beautiful you on the computer screen before paying any fees or undergoing surgery"—advertisement for cosmetic surgery clinic.

"Look and Feel Great! Total Bust Beautifier Exercises . . . featuring the Cleavage Enhancer"—title of magazine article.

"Turn your no body into a great body"—title of magazine article.

"Inside every skin there's a more beautiful skin wait-ing to get out!"—advertisement for skin-care product.

No doubt about it, Americans are obsessed with physical attractiveness. Television, films, magazine and newspaper ads, are filled primarily with beautiful people. We admire attractive people. We try to be like them as we spend billions of dollars trying to make ourselves look more attractive. Our society seems almost to worship beauty.

We have already seen that possession of social skills is a powerful force leading to success in social interaction and an ability to influence others. But when we combine the power of social skills with the power of physical attractiveness, we get a tremendous increase in charisma potential.

Since we tend to value physical attractiveness so highly, beautiful people have certain advantages in day-to-day social life. Research has shown that good-looking persons are better liked in initial meetings than are un-attractive persons.[1] Moreover, attractive people tend to be blessed with what is called the "halo effect,"[2] which is the assumption that simply because physically attractive persons possess a highly valued characteristic—their beauty—we also tend to believe that they possess other valued attributes. Good-looking persons are thus seen as more sociable and outgoing, kind, honest, talented, and intelligent. Attractive persons are also more desirable as dating partners or possible marriage partners.[3]

If you ask people what they find alluring about others, they are likely to come up with a wide range of different characteristics. Attractiveness will be mentioned, but people will also claim to be interested in others who are bright, energetic, kind, and those who have a "great personality." Although we may believe that there are a number of features that attract us to a prospective partner, in the initial stages of attraction, the effect of physical appearance seems to be of overwhelming importance. In one study, college students were rated on physical attractiveness as they purchased tickets for a dance. At the dance, they were randomly paired with partners of the opposite sex. During the dance the students were asked to fill out a questionnaire about their partner. They were asked specifically how much they liked the person and whether they would like to go out with this person in the future. The results indicated that only physical attractiveness predicted whether students liked and wanted to continue seeing the partner. Personality, intelligence, and other factors did not matter at all.[4] Physical attractiveness does indeed seem to be a powerful force in capturing the attention and interest of others.

What makes a person physically attractive? Of course, standards of physical attractiveness vary from culture to culture and across periods of time. One need only compare the rotund women depicted in seventeenth-century paintings with the sleek models pictured in today's health-spa ads to realize that standards of female body attractiveness can change drastically over time. However, the attractiveness of certain physical characteristics may remain quite stable. For example, extremely large noses or ears, very close-set eyes, and rough pockmarked complexions might always be considered unattractive.

Physical attractiveness, rather than being a single characteristic, is actually a constellation of many things. Facial features, size and proportions of body parts, hair quality and style, posture, use of makeup, and mode of dress are all visual components of attractiveness. Some of these, especially hairstyle, dress, and cosmetic use, are fairly easily altered to make us more or less attractive.

Others are more difficult to change. To some extent, an unattractive, flabby body can be made more attractive through disciplined exercise and weight training. Plastic surgery can make facial features more attractive, although at considerable cost and some pain and discomfort.

Fortunately, there is more to physical attractiveness than just static, visual qualities. Our manner and style of behavior—the things that we say and do—can make us more or less attractive. The *way* that we say or do things, our nonverbal behavior, also contributes to attractiveness.

Charisma and physical attractiveness are inextricably bound. People who are born beautiful may initially have a slight edge. By developing their social skills, beautiful people can become charismatic. On the other hand, persons less blessed by inherited looks can develop their social skills and charisma and thus make themselves more attractive to others.

Many of our famous charismatic persons are beautiful women and handsome men—the Kennedys, the Elizabeth Taylors, and Robert Redfords. Others, such as Humphrey Bogart, Mahatma Gandhi, and Eleanor Roosevelt, were not classic beauties at all, yet they still had charisma.

There are essentially two types of attractiveness. The first is *static* physical attractiveness. It refers to the more stable, visual components of attractiveness—facial features, body size and proportions, hairstyle, and makeup. This is the attractiveness that can be seen in a photograph. Static physical attractiveness is what people commonly refer to as beauty.

The second type is *dynamic* attractiveness and refers to the changing behavioral components of attractiveness. The grace with which persons move, their expressive style, the positive qualities of the voice, the rhythm and timing of speech, all contribute to dynamic attractiveness. Of these two types of attractiveness, the latter is most likely to be affected by the possession of social skills. Thus, charismatic, socially skilled individuals can transcend the limitations of static characteristics of beauty and make themselves more attractive through dynamic qualities. Humphrey Bogart was not a clasically handsome man by any means. Yet, he was able to emit cues of masculine sexuality that made him extremely attractive to many women. Similarly, Liza Minelli has an alluring sensuality and passion in her movements on stage that rise above the fact that she lacks the facial features of a cover girl. Research on physical attractiveness and the general public's thinking about attractiveness have concentrated primarily on static attractiveness. Dynamic attractiveness has been largely overlooked. However, it is important that attention be given to dynamic attractiveness, for this is most often used by charismatic individuals to draw others to them.

While much of static physical attractiveness is with us at birth, dynamic physical attractiveness is acquired. People can learn to behave in ways that will make them more attractive to others. Scarlett O'Hara, in Margaret Mitchell's *Gone with the Wind* illustrates dynamic attractiveness. As the author describes her, Scarlett O'Hara is not stunningly beautiful. She does, however, know how to make herself appealing to men. Scarlett flirts, giggles, behaves seductively, and knows all of the "tricks" to use to capture the hearts of her suitors.

While most of Scarlett's dynamic attractiveness stems from her expressive, coquettish qualities, she is also keenly aware of social rules and patterns of "typical" male behavior. By bending social rules and triggering certain predictable responses in her suitors, Scarlett is able to make herself even more alluring.

One of the more interesting aspects of dynamic physical attractiveness is how quickly it can be turned on or off, as the character of Scarlett O'Hara shows. When there are eligible men nearby, she turns on her flirtatious charms.

A clever experiment conducted by University of Minnesota researchers showed that dynamic attractiveness could be stimulated by the behavior of others.[6] In this study, male and female college students were asked to get acquainted through a telephone conversation. Each man was given a photograph of the woman he was supposedly talking to. Actually, the photograph was of either a very attractive or a very unattractive woman, not a photo of the person to whom they were actually talking. The telephone conversations were tape recorded, with male and female voices put on separate tapes. Groups of judges listened to the tape recordings and made ratings of the attractiveness of the voices of the men and women. The judges rated the men who thought they were talking to an attractive woman as more attractive, sexually warm, interesting, and sociable than the men who believed they were talking to an unattractive woman. In other words, men who thought they were talking to an attractive woman became more dynamically attractive themselves.

But the most remarkable finding concerned the changes that occurred in the women's behavior. Women who were talking to a man who believed they were attractive also began to behave in more dynamically attractive ways. The judges rated them as more poised, outgoing, and likable than the women whose partners thought that they were actually unattractive. To summarize, the men were attempting to behave in an attractive fashion to impress the supposedly attractive female on the other end of the line. The men's behavior, in turn, called forth attractive behavior in the women. Interestingly, both the men and women in this experiment were rated by judges as being more sociable and socially adept—further indication that social skills and dynamic attractiveness are closely linked.

CHARISMA AND INITIAL ATTRACTION

In a series of studies, we have tried to investigate how people come to be more or less attractive to others and the role that charisma and social skills play in making persons more attractive.

In the first of these studies, we secretly videotaped persons who were arriving to take part in a psychology experiment. The hidden videocamera recorded each person as he or she entered the laboratory and was greeted by the experimenter. The experimenter gave a brief description of the experiment and asked the subject some simple questions. Only the first few moments of this initial encounter were videotaped. A week before, all subjects had completed the ACT questionnaire. We then showed the videotapes to two groups of judges. The first group watched the videotaped initial interactions and simply rated each subject's physical attractiveness. The second group of judges was asked to watch the tapes and indicate how much they liked or disliked each person.

As we expected, the halo effect was found. Physically attractive persons were rated as more likable than unattractive persons. When we looked at the ACT scores and the likability ratings, we found that expressive persons also made more favorable impressions on our judges. Most importantly, when we examined the effects of attractiveness and expressiveness simultaneously, we found that some of the effects were independent. That is, expressiveness contributed to a person's likability regardless of whether he or she was attractive or unattractive. Attractive persons tended to make more favorable impressions, but if they lacked beauty, they were able to compensate with dynamic expressivity. Of course, the most likable persons in initial encounters tended to be those who possessed both static and dynamic attractiveness.

Our next experiment involved a slightly longer interaction. In this case, subjects were also surreptitiously videotaped while they entered a laboratory to participate in an experiment. Prior to the experiment, the subjects had filled out the Social Skills Inventory. Again, each subject was greeted at the door by the experimenter who instructed him to "go over and introduce yourself to the other two people who will be participating in this experiment with you." Seated nearby were a young man and woman who were evidently also participants in the experiment. Actually, the two persons were research assistants who were instructed to behave in the same manner with each subject. They were told to ask each subject the same simple questions. The experimenter left the room an the three participants conversed for a short while. The experimenter then returned, turned off the videotape recorder, and took a photograph of the subject. After the subject left, the experimenter and the two research assistants separately rated how much they liked the subject. In order to get a measure of static attractiveness, the subjects' photographs were shown to a group of judges, who rated each on a scale of physical attractiveness. An additional group of judges was shown the videotaped interactions and asked to rate how much they liked each of the subjects.

In this longer interaction, physical attractiveness, as judged from the photographs, was only slightly related to how well-liked each subject was. However, scores on the expressive scales of the Social Skills Inventory, and their total SSI score for charisma potential, were all related to the likability ratings given to each subject by both the "live" judges (the experimenter and research assistants) and the judges who watched the interactions on videotape. But the strongest predictor of how well-liked the subjects were in this longer interaction was the score on the social-control scale of the SSI. In other words, persons who were skilled at social role-playing received the most favorable evaluations. Again, static attractiveness and dynamic, expressive skills led to positive initial impressions. But individuals who were skilled conversationalists (i.e., high scorers on social control), particularly in this situation, which involved a meeting of total strangers, were the most liked of all. The results of these studies indicate that it is the possession of social skills—charisma potential—that is behind dynamic attractiveness.

In a final study, we examined what the subjects in the experiments did to make themselves dynamically attractive—the types of expressive behavior that they emitted in these brief meetings. In order to do this, we again tabulated a large number and variety of nonverbal and vocal cues, following the same "content analysis" procedure that was used in the videotaped studies of deception mentioned in Chapter 3. Initially, we had somewhat complex results that were difficult to interpret. However, when we examined male and female subjects separately, things became much clearer. The behaviors that men used to make themselves dynamically attractive were quite different than the cues that women used. Specifically, if a male subject spoke at a rapid and fluent pace, and emphasized the speech with gestures and body movements, he was rated more favorably by our judges. Women, on the other hand, expressed dynamic attractiveness through changes in their facial expressions. But speech and body-movement cues did not greatly affect the dynamic attractiveness of women subjects in our study. Similarly, facial expressiveness was unrelated to dynamic attractiveness in men. In short, the dynamically attractive cues for men and for women seem to be quite different. Women made themselves more attractive through attractive-looking facial expressions. Men who were considered more dynamically attractive did so through gestures and body movements.[7]

These studies indicate that static physical attractiveness is important in the earliest stages of an interaction. Of course. We value physical attractiveness greatly, and our attention and interest are immediately drawn to beauty when we see it. But expressiveness—attractive, dynamic movement—is also attention-getting and favorably received in these initial stages. But what happens as the relationship progresses beyond the initial stages? What role do attractiveness and expressiveness play in long-term relationships?

The evidence suggests that the importance of physical attractiveness diminishes as a relationship progresses. Attractiveness plays an important part in gaining our attention and interest, but as we begin to find out more about the person with whom we are interacting, we look for other qualities. Is this person articulate (social expressivity)? Is he cultured, refined, and courteous (social sensitivity and social control)? Is this individual sensitive and responsive to my feelings? Do I feel comfortable with her (emotional sensitivity and emotional control)?

Does he truly understand what I am saying and feeling (social sensitivity and emotional sensitivity)? As the interaction continues, and a relationship develops, the other basic social skills become very important.

When it comes to the development of a long-term attraction—a meaningful and deep relationship between individuals—a number of social skills are important. People who are attractive and emotionally expressive, without possessing the required sensitivity and regulatory social skills, are all "flash" and no substance. Our initial fascination with them dies quickly, like the effects of a fireworks display. But the charismatic person continues to hold our attraction, and a deep attachment can develop.

While it is clear that skill in nonverbal communication plays a very important role in the development of a friendship or dating relationship, verbal abilities are also important. To attract the interest of another person, it is important to say the kinds of things that will continue to hold the other person's attention and make him or her want to get to know you better. It is also important that the topics discussed are appropriate to the social situations and that they do not violate any social rules. Here again, possession of a balance of the basic social skills underlying charisma is the key to success.

Several years ago, a very popular book was available through a mail-order publisher. The book concerned how to "pick up" women. (Of course it was followed by other books on how to pick up men, and sequels telling you what to do with them once you got them.) As an extra, added bonus the order would include a list of the "100 greatest opening lines." Opening lines are often very important because of what are called "snap judgments." People have a tendency to make an overall evaluation of a person from the first few moments of an initial encounter. What a person says, particularly in the initial stages of an interaction, can often determine whether the interaction will continue and where it may eventually lead.

I recall accompanying a friend to several parties. My friend was single and interested in meeting women, but he had difficulty in conversing with strangers, particularly female strangers. My friend was a veterinarian, which should have been a natural and easy topic for conversation. At these parties, women would seem genuinely interested when first hearing of his profession, and they would encourage him to talk about his work. I assume that these women expected to hear sweet stories of his healing sick puppies and kittens. Unfortunately, my friend worked exclusively with farm animals. He would immediately go into a discussion of the artificial insemination of cows or the eradication of certain sheep parasites— hardly the topics the ladies expected to hear. I would watch painfully as his audience would excuse themselves and move on.

My veterinarian friend lacked social sensitivity and social control. He needed to be aware of the appropriate topics of conversation at a particular social gathering and the audience to whom he was speaking. He also needed to monitor his conversation in order to avoid saying things that might be considered offensive or saying things that would put himself in a bad light, particularly in the initial stages of an interaction. In a later conversation, once the participants had gotten to know one another, his veterinary work might seem fascinating.

Our research has shown that charismatic, socially skilled persons more easily develop friendships and dating relationships than do persons low in social skills. Socially skilled persons are also less likely to describe themselves as shy than are unskilled individuals. Therefore, socially skilled persons tend to have large social networks—friends to socialize with, and acquaintances who they can try to get to know better. Thus, it seems that people with charisma potential are more likely to meet potential romantic partners, and their social skills will help to develop and maintain love relationships.

CHARISMA, SOCIAL SKILLS, AND THE DEVELOPMENT OF LASTING RELATIONSHIPS

We have already discussed the role that expressive skills play in ability to attract the interest of others in casual interactions, but what is the part that charisma and social skills play in more long-term relationships?

According to psychologists George Levinger and J. Snoek,[8] relationships develop in a series of stages. In the first stage, individuals simply become aware of each other. As we have seen, physical attractiveness and emotional expressivity play an important part in capturing the awareness of others. The second stage involves *surface contact*. This involves casual first conversations— opening lines, polite banter, and finding out basic information about the person's occupation, interests, and hobbies. It is in this second stage that skill in social expressivity is critical. As you recall, social expressivity involves speaking ability.

As the budding relationship moves to the deepest level, the stage of *mutuality*, the two individuals begin to spend more time together and explore each other. A critical process at this stage is called "self-disclosure." Through self-disclosure, people begin to reveal personal information about themselves. As the relationship moves to deeper levels of mutuality, disclosure becomes more intimate. Private beliefs, hopes, and dreams are shared, as well as feelings for each other. Both verbal and non-verbal expressions of affection are exchanged. The social skills of expressivity and sensitivity are extremely important if the mutual process of exchange of private information is to flow smoothly and evenly. As the relationship develops further, the persons involved may move from feelings of liking to feelings of love.

PASSIONATE LOVE AND COMPANIONATE LOVE

Elaine Hatfield and William Walster[9] distinguish between two types of love: *passionate* love and *companionate* love. Passionate love is fiery and emotional. It is the kind of

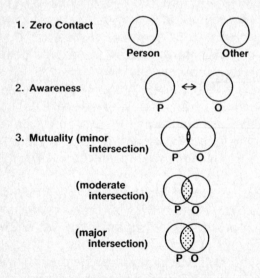

Levels of relationship between two people.
(Adapted from Levinger, 1980.)

love that poets and songwriters refer to as a burning desire for another. Passionate love is the erotic, emotional spirit of a love relationship. On the other hand, companionate love results from deep friendship and commitment. If two people are to remain together for many years in a healthy, sharing relationship, the presence of companionate love is of the utmost importance. Ideally, both should be present for a relationship to last the test of time.

Many relationships typically begin with feelings of passion. Two people are physically attracted to each other, and the flames of passionate love begin to burn. If the relationship is to develop into something permanent, companionate love must also emerge. In one study, women married for more than thirty three years reported feeling a great deal of companionate love for their mates and lesser, but significant, amounts of passionate love, indicating that companionate love is most necessary for the relationship to endure.[10] Passionate love alone is not usually sufficient for long-term relationships, for passionate love is primarily based on sexual compatibility. Passionate love may burn out in a relatively short time. In many cases, people are initially attracted to one another by feelings of passion. However, as the couple spends more and more time together, they may be unable to develop a good, working friendship. If the passion begins to die, the relationship will usually end. To spend their lives together, two people must be compatible on many levels, not only on the physical level. They must be able to deal with the trials and tribulations of everyday life in a true partnership. Companionate love seems crucial.

While companionate love alone might be sufficient for certain lasting relationships, a marriage based solely on companionate love lacks that healthy emotional spark that is the hallmark of passionate love. The key to a truly rewarding lasting relationship is deep companionate love in a partnership that strives to keep the passion alive.

Since passionate love can sometimes die quickly, and since companionate love may be slow to develop, the best strategy for insuring a long-term relationship may be to begin with companionate love. In certain rare instances, a deep friendship based on companionate love may suddenly develop a spark of passion and a romantic, lasting relationship, based on both kinds of love, may be the end product.

How do these two types of love relate to charisma and social skills? If you remember, we mentioned earlier that emotional communication is a ``primitive'' form of communication, inherited from our earliest ancestors. The use of language and the rules governing civilized social behavior represent modern advancements in human communication. The development of passionate love depends greatly on the communication of emotions between the couple. Expression of feelings is at the heart of passionate love. Thus, skills in emotional communication, particularly emotional expressivity and emotional sensitivity, play an important role in the development of passionate love. Social communication skills are critical to the development of companionate love. It is through verbal exchange that we learn about the innermost thoughts of those we love. Moreover, a lifelong committment is also dependent on a very complex process of social exchange—learning to give and take. Advice is given and taken, decisions are made and accepted, shows of support are provided and requested. The ability to carry out these important social exchanges, and to keep the give-and-take process in balance, is greatly dependent on the communication skills of the couple involved.

Social skills are very often the ties that bind persons together in long-term, loving relationships.

Thus far, we have examined the basic components of charisma—the six dimensions of social skill: emotional and social expressivity, sensitivity, and social control. We have seen how charisma is related to physical attractiveness and how charisma can be used to draw others to the charismatic person. In the next section, we will begin to see how the charismatic person uses social skills to influence others and to lead them to action.

❦ II ❦

Charisma: How It Is Used

5

Charisma, Leadership, and Political Power

THE CHARISMATIC LEADER

Clearly, the greatest interest in charisma has been in the area of leadership. Virtually all of the early research on charisma, and much popular speculation, has focused on charismatic leaders of political or religious movements. Many of our examples of charismatic persons are themselves well-known leaders.

It was the German sociologist Max Weber who first developed the concept of the charismatic leader. Weber stated that the charismatic leader possesses extraordinary qualities that make him attractive to potential followers:

> The term of charisma will be applied to a certain quality of the individual personality by virtue of which he is set apart from ordinary men and treated as endowed with supernatural, superhuman, or at least exceptional powers and qualities.[1]

By our definition, the charismatic person's "exceptional qualities" refer to the possession of highly-developed social skills, also known as charisma potential. But according to Weber, these exceptional beings become charismatic leaders only when the situation is right. The leader must have followers, and the followers must be strongly devoted to the leader. The group must also have a cause, some reason for existence and for taking action. Weber saw charismatic leadership as a revolutionary force leading to social change and the creation of new institutions. Charismatic warriors such as Julius Caesar and Napoleon lead to the creation of empires. Charismatic spiritual leaders such as Jesus Christ and Mohammed direct followers to develop new religions. Charismatic statesmen and politicians such as Lenin and David Ben-Gurion lead to the formation of new nations or governments.

Yet, we know that not all powerful leaders are charismatic. Members of royal families accede the throne by virtue of birth rather than through the possession of any leadership or charismatic qualities. An individual may become a leader due to some important skill that a group values—a skill totally unrelated to the communication skills that are the underlying components of charisma.

In the same vein, only a small percentage of charismatic persons are likely to rise to powerful leadership positions. Luck, timing, the fickleness of potential followers, and a host of other factors all play a role in determining who will rise to positions of leadership. However, on those occasions when a socially skilled, charismatic individual is able to attain a position of power and authority, the results can be dramatic and forceful.

Soon after John F. Kennedy received the Democratic nomination for President in 1960, the force of his charismatic presence began to unfold as crowds of followers gathered to see him.

> For the crowds that erupted to greet Kennedy in the streets and squares of the Northeast in the last few weeks of the campaign were, and remain, unbelievable . . . the Kennedy crowds were spectacular. It was not the numbers that made them spectacular . . . but their frenzied quality.
>
> One remembers being in a Kennedy crowd and suddenly sensing far off on the edge of it a ripple of pressure beginning, and the ripple, which always started at the back, would grow like a wave, surging forward as it gathered strength, until it would squeeze the front rank of the crowd against the wooden barricade . . . and thousands of bodies would, helplessly but ecstatically, be locked in the rhythmic back-and-forth rocking.[2]

The power of the charismatic leader was also evident during Martin Luther King's speech to the participants of the 1963 Freedom March on Washington.

> Two hundred and fifty thousand people applauded thunderously, and voiced in a sort of chant, *Martin Luther King* . . . He started out with the written speech, delivering it with great eloquence . . . When he got to the

rhythmic part of demanding freedom *now,* and wanting jobs *now,* the crowd caught the timing and shouted *now* in cadence. Their response lifted Martin in a surge of emotion to new heights of inspiration. Abandoning his written speech, forgetting time, he spoke from his heart, his voice soaring magnificently out over that crowd and over to all the world. It seemed to all of us there that day that his words flowed from some higher place, through Martin, to the weary people before him. Yea—Heaven itself opened up and we all seemed transformed.[3]

As illustrated here, the charismatic leader inspires the crowd, but he also becomes charged by the emotions of the followers. Thus, there is an interplay between leader and followers that helps to build a strong union between them. While the leader has control and influence over followers, the charismatic leader also responds to the needs and desires of the group. It is a two-way relationship.

CHARISMA PROFILE: JOHN FITZGERALD KENNEDY

About the Charisma Profiles: These profiles of charismatic persons are for illustrative purposes only. They are designed to show how the various basic social skills combine to create different types of charismatic personalities. The ratings of the basic skill dimensions are derived from writings about famous charismatic individuals, accounts from persons who knew them, and from the author's observations of films.

John F. Kennedy, in many people's minds, was the epitome of the charismatic politician—handsome, youthful, intelligent, and (most importantly) a brilliant communicator. JFK possessed tremendous levels of basic social skills and a great deal of balance among the skills. Kennedy's major strengths were in the verbal skill areas of social expressivity, social sensitivity, and social control. He was a a brilliant speaker and author of words and he spoke with a rapid-fire delivery. Kennedy was also an outstanding listener. He exuded self-confidence, derived primarily from his early upbringing and extensive early life experiences (e.g., military, foreign travel, political heritage, education). But perhaps Kennedy's greatest strength was his extraordinary emotional control. John Kennedy seemed to be a "personality under control, this insistence on distancing himself from displays of emotion."

"[He] concealed anguish under a mask of courtesy and composure."[4]

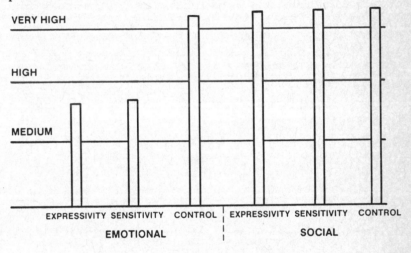

CHARISMA PROFILE: ROBERT FRANCIS KENNEDY

Robert F. Kennedy was highly skilled in all of the basic charisma components. However, in contrast to John's exceptional verbal/

social skills, Robert's greatest strengths were in the areas of emotional expressivity and sensitivity. The behavior of John Kennedy was carefully planned and controlled. Robert was more spontaneous, often governed by his feelings.

> John Kennedy was urbane, objective, analytical, controlled, contained, masterful, a man of perspective; Robert, while very bright and increasingly reflective, was more open, exposed, emotional, subjective, intense, a man of commitment.[5]

Sensitive, concerned and compassionate, Robert Kennedy was moved by the plight of disadvantaged groups, but was quick to anger against those persons who treated others unfairly and preyed on the unfortunate. Shy as a child, and not a great speaker, Robert Kennedy learned to compensate by filling his speeches with passion and by building strong, emotional friendships.

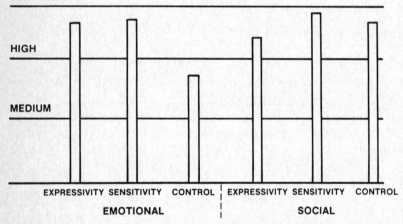

TASKS OF THE CHARISMATIC LEADER

The charismatic leader is thoroughly dependent on followers. It is the deep bond between the charismatic leader and his supporters that holds the charismatic leader in power. But it is a sometimes precarious relationship, with the communication skills of the leader playing a major role in keeping him in power. The charismatic leader must also perform certain crucial tasks in order to maintain the leadership role. If the charismatic leader fails to accomplish these tasks, his hold on the followers may dissipate and the leader can fall from power.

The first task of the charismatic leader is *to rouse followers to action*. This involves stirring up the emotions and consciousness of potential followers. Most typically, the charismatic leader uses expressive skills to incite followers to states of anger, bravery, or indignation.

In his stirring address following the Japanese bombing of Pearl Harbor, Franklin Delano Roosevelt roused an entire nation to a concerted and passionate effort to combat a new enemy.

> Everywhere across the land, Americans gathered before their radios listening to the familiar voice, which spoke with great deliberation:
>
> "Yesterday, December 7, 1941—a date which will live in infamy—the United States was suddenly and deliberately attacked by naval and air forces of the Empire of Japan . . . With confidence in our armed forces . . . with the unbounding determination of our people—we will gain the inevitable triumph—so help us God."

The charismatic President, who had led a nation out of a devastating Depression, was now assuming the helm in a new crisis. Throughout his presidency, Roosevelt and the United States constantly faced some sort of crisis situation. These crises served the function of bringing leader and followers together in a concerted effort to overcome the threat. Following the destruction of the United States fleet at Pearl Harbor, and as the early defeats of the war continued, Roosevelt continually appealed to the American people to rally their resources to fight the enemy.

> Roosevelt's confident optimism shone like a beacon in the gloom of defeat. He was constantly on the radio, reporting on the progress of the fighting and making certain that the American people never wavered in their determination to fight through to victory.
> "No matter what our enemies . . . in their desperation may attempt to do to us—we will say as the people of London have said, 'We can take it' . . . And what's more, we can give it back—with compound interest."[6]

Although we usually imagine charismatic leaders inciting crowds to violent or aggressive action against foes, charismatic leaders have also proven capable of inspiring followers to *nonviolent* action. In the early 1930's, Mahatma Gandhi led India in a unified movement of nonviolence designed to shake off the yoke of oppression by the ruling British government. At Gandhi's urging, rich and poor Indians alike banded together to fight British oppression, not through violence, but through peaceful collective action, through boycotting British goods, and by refusing to follow government orders.

> The boycott of foreign cloth became almost universal, many Indians quit their government jobs, many more refused to pay taxes, and all over the country women from aristocratic and middle-class homes marched on picket lines protesting the sale of English textiles.[7]

The ability of Gandhi to rouse followers to nonviolent action was perhaps most dramatically portrayed in the

Salt Marches. The British government had imposed a heavy tax on salt and had restricted Indians from gathering it, requiring that salt be purchased only from heavily taxed government sources. In an act of civil disobedience, Gandhi led followers to the seashore to gather salt. The marchers were thoroughly instilled with Gandhi's doctrine of nonviolence.

> On May 21, a column of more than two hundred . . . advanced on the great salt pans. Facing them were four hundred Surat policemen, commanded by six British officers . . . Suddenly, at a word of command scores of native policemen rushed upon the advancing marchers and rained blows on their heads with their steel-shod *lathis* (sticks). Not one of the marchers even raised an arm to fend off the blows. They went down like tenpins . . . The survivors, without breaking ranks, silently and doggedly marched on until struck down . . . They marched steadily with heads up, without the encouragement of music or cheering or any possibility that they might escape injury or death . . . It seemed that they were thoroughly imbued with Gandhi's nonviolence creed, and the leaders constantly stood in front of the ranks imploring them to remember that Gandhi's soul was with them.[8]

Definitely, the ability to rouse followers to action is a crucial element for the charismatic leader. As Arthur Schweitzer states in his *Theory of Political Charisma:*

> Controlled passions are thus as important as exceptional deeds to engender the indispensable confidence of the followers in the political leader . . . In possessing the power to arouse ecstasies, he generates the enthusiasm of the masses and derives power from their emotional attachment to him.[9]

The second task of the charismatic leader is *to serve as a symbol of worship and admiration*. In some instances, the charismatic leader is the rallying point for the followers' devotion and loyalty to the cause. In other cases, the followers' allegiance may be given directly to the leader and may involve blind support of whatever course the leader decides to take.

Regardless of the reason for followers' initial support, the charismatic leader often becomes an object of deep devotion for many of the disciples. The leader is revered and placed on a pedestal. To maintain this charismatic appeal, the leader needs to remain untarnished in the eyes of the followers. The leader must continue to display extraordinary qualities (e.g., exceptional devotion to the cause, superhuman strength to endure suffering or sacrifice), actions that set him apart from his followers.

T. E. Lawrence, better known as Lawrence of Arabia, was the charismatic leader of the Arab revolt against the Turks during World War I. An Englishman, Lawrence was able to gain the confidence of the Arab warriors through his extreme dedication to their cause. In order to prove himself to the Arab leaders, Lawrence endured many hardships. He exposed himself to incredible risks during battle, endured pain and thirst on long marches through the desert, and adapted himself to the Arab way of life. Many times during the revolt, Lawrence proved himself a charismatic leader as he rallied the warriors, urging them on to greater efforts:

> Lawrence was true Arab now, preaching with a prophetic eloquence the gospel of revolt. Its glory, he urged, lay in bitterness and suffering, and the sacrifice of the body to the spirit . . . The Serahin (an Arab tribe) listened entranced; their worldliness vanished and before daylight

came they were swearing to ride with Lawrence any-where.[10]

The charismatic leader often engages in *impression management*—carefully controlling outward appearance—to cover up any personal weaknesses in an effort to continue receiving the group's respect, admiration, and support. It is here that the leader's skill in social control, or his role-playing ability, is called into play. The leader gives careful consideration to appearance and how his behavior may be interpreted by others. He behaves in a manner that is deemed socially appropriate by the group as a whole. Behavior that is considered inappropriate may arouse suspicion in followers; behavior that is clearly considered bizarre or immoral may cause the charismatic leader to fall from grace and run the risk of losing much of his charismatic appeal. For example, Ted Kennedy's Chappaquiddick incident led to the tarnishing of his image, a great loss of popularity, and may have cost him the presidency.

In order to maintain an untarnished image, the charismatic leader may attempt to remain distanced from supporters. Personal contacts are limited to only a small inner circle of highly trusted and devoted disciples. When the leader does make an appearance before the general crowds of followers, it is usually in a carefully controlled and staged presentation. For example, an audience with the Pope usually involves a brief and physically distant encounter, one that is governed by ceremony. Political leaders present themselves to the public with a prepared speech or in a carefully staged press conference—usually one in which answers to certain questions have been prepared beforehand and the appropriate type of questions may have even been planted with members of the audience. The effects of this distancing can make a charismatic leader—a person who already possesses extraordinary communicative powers—seem larger than life, an object worthy of devotion.

However, the charismatic leader must be sure that this distancing is not too great. Distance between leader and followers must be carefully regulated to maintain charismatic appeal. The leader must keep some contact with followers, for it is through the charismatic leader's presence that the crowd becomes inspired and energized. Charismatic U.S. President Theodore Roosevelt was especially aware of the impact that his presence had on followers. He was a tireless campaigner, crisscrossing the country, making speeches from the back of a train, in order to maintain the support of followers. In this way, Roosevelt could "touch" as many supporters as possible, even if his presence was fleeting. As a New York politician observed:

> He spoke about ten minutes—the speech was nothing, but the man's presence was everything. It was electrical, magnetic. I looked in the faces of hundreds and saw only pleasure and satisfaction. When the train moved away, scores of men and women ran after the train, waving hats and handkerchiefs and cheering, trying to keep him in sight as long as possible.[11]

The third task of the charismatic leader is *to lead the group to successful attainment of goals.* It is here that the leader's sensitivity plays a crucial role. He must be aware of, and responsive to, his followers' needs. To maintain the position of power, a charismatic leader needs to demonstrate some successes or gains for the group. Franklin Delano Roosevelt's long and firm hold on the presidency may have been due partly to raising the standard of living for most Americans and the successful U.S. intervention in the Second World War. Similarly, Ronald Reagan's popularity may be attributable to the general perception that he has stimulated economic growth and has "gotten America moving again."

To remain in power, it is important that the leader continually demonstrate that he is successful in achieving some of the group's goals. Today's national leaders leap at every opportunity to show that their leadership and their administrations are successful. Indicators of economic growth, unemployment indexes, and polls of popular support (if favorable) are seized by the leader and exhibited as evidence of success. In a very human type of reaction, world leaders will also try to avoid taking blame when such indexes are discouraging. A hurried scramble may take place to find the "true" cause of the downturn, and certain persons or groups may be used as scapegoats to take the burden of failure away from the leader. In recent U.S. presidential administrations, certain cabinet members have played these scapegoat roles. When the administration is faced with some failure, a cabinet member, or some other chief official, may resign in an effort to direct blame away from the President, (e.g., resignation of various Reagan administration officials during the "Irangate" scandal). It is crucial that the charismatic leader avoid failure, for in extreme instances the leader's failures can have devastating consequences.

Benito Mussolini was a popular and seemingly charismatic leader of the Italian people, as long as his military escapades and domestic programs were perceived as successful, or at least as nondamaging. However, after a series of terrible defeats at the hands of the Allied forces, with accompanying economic drains on the country, Mussolini quickly fell from grace, was ousted from power, and was eventually killed by his own people. Even a leader with tremendous charisma will have difficulty maintaining a hold on followers in the face of defeat.

Because followers place tremendous faith in their leader, should he fail in the task of leading the group to the attainment of goals, the leader often becomes the focal point for blame. However, should the leader die while trying to attain the goals, he may be held blameless and may insure his place of honor and reverence in the group's history.

CHARISMA AND THE MARTYRED LEADER

Some charismatic leaders are killed during their reigns of leadership, many at the peak of their popularity and power—John Kennedy, Robert Kennedy, Gandhi, Martin Luther King, Jr., Anwar Sadat. These leaders are thus seen by their followers as martyrs for their causes, and their status as charismatic leaders is preserved for history. The charismatic leaders who die for their causes (or who die while still maintaining some charismatic hold on followers as did Eva Peron and Franklin Delano Roosevelt) are likely to remain figures imbued with charisma. They are immediately and permanently distanced from their followers. While living leaders may run the risk of losing some of their charismatic power due to human error, the charisma of martyred leaders usually remains and may have some effect on followers even after death. Typically, when a charismatic leader dies, there is some turmoil. Mass outpourings of affection and loyalty are common. In certain cases, as in the riots following the death of Martin Luther King, Jr., followers may feel frustrated and lash out at real or imagined enemies. Vows to carry on the work of the slain leader may be made. But the charismatic leader's strength lays in his power to communicate. Thus, the hold that the leader has on followers often dissipates after his death.

Historically, however, the martyred charismatic leader may rise to a figure of mythic proportions as followers selectively remember the positive attributes of the leader and tend to forget weaknesses. Loyal followers may speculate on the triumphs the leader might have accomplished had he or she been spared the assassin's bullet or the fatal disease. The leader's successor may have difficulty establishing his or her own charismatic power because the successor is continually contrasted with the martyred leader, and the successor pales in comparison. By virtue of martyrdom, the late leader's weaknesses are often forgotten or overlooked while the successor is laden with human frailties. Perhaps this contrast is responsible for the inability of many successors of assassinated charismatic leaders to themselves achieve charismatic leadership status in spite of their own personal accomplishments, communication effectiveness, and public appeal.

A CASE STUDY IN UNCHARISMATIC LEADERSHIP: THE FAILURE OF RICHARD NIXON

In order to understand fully the qualities and abilities of the charismatic leader, it is important to examine leaders who are not particularly charismatic as well. Many times during the course of our charisma research, we have asked people to name famous charismatic persons. We have also asked them to list noncharismatic individuals. One famous leader who often makes the noncharismatic list is Richard Nixon. It is important to emphasize that while Nixon is most definitely not a charismatic figure, he is by no means completely lacking in social skills (i.e., he is not the "opposite" of charismatic). Richard Nixon is an above-average communicator. He would not have been able to attain his many high-level political positions without being an effective and skilled communicator. But many factors contribute to Nixon's noncharismatic image.

First and foremost, Nixon is viewed as a failure. The folly of Watergate, the bungled cover-up, and his subsequent resignation insure his place in history as a leader who failed.

Secondly, because of his defeat in the 1960 presidential election, Nixon was doomed to continual comparisons to John Kennedy. In the most famous of televised debates, Kennedy emerged as a winning charismatic figure, while Nixon appeared a much less effective communicator. Nixon was a victim of what psychologists call the "contrast effect." Against another noncharismatic opponent, Nixon, a proven debater and politician, might have fared better. Perhaps in a forum other than television—with its emphasis on close-ups and short time allotments that favored Kennedy's physical attractiveness and rapid-fire delivery—Nixon might have emerged as the victor and changed the course of history.[12]

Finally, Nixon was, by his own admission, deficient in certain crucial social skills. In particular, he lacked emotional expressivity and social control—two skills that are imperative for charismatic leadership.

> Perhaps my major liability—and this may sound incongruous—that I am essentially shyer than the usually

extrovert politician ought to be . . . I have a great liking for the plain people, but I feel ill at ease with the prominent.[13]

From Nixon's earliest days, and throughout his political career, only an inner circle of friends was able to get close to him.

> Nixon was the sort of young man who impressed relatives and various teachers by his ability to produce the "right" answers and by his bright, hardworking ways. Nixon's classmates also had high regard for his diligence and capability, but most of them were not drawn to him as a person, and his circle of friends was small even then. Within this circle, Nixon gave and received the kind of loyalty that would become a hallmark of his political existence. Outside his circle, however, his reserve appeared as arrogance, and his aloofness, coldness. He always commanded respect. Rarely did he inspire the human affection that Americans often associate with their Presidents.[14]

Richard Nixon's successes were due to his intelligence, persistence, and drive rather than to any superior skills as a statesman or a spokesman arousing the people. Nixon had a tendency to undercommunicate—to keep his feelings to himself.

> Rarely could Nixon express his own love for others or for country in a way that similarly aroused the emotions of others . . . The most misplaced quality of this private, public man was that he lacked the gift to say on stage what he saw in his heart.[15]

Nixon lacked many of the components of charisma. He was unable to arouse the passions of his audience. His political successes were most likely attributable to his followers' identification with him as one of their own—the common man—and to his political longevity, than to any inspirational leadership qualities. As we have seen, a charismatic leader must be emotionally expressive. Nixon was not.

Nixon was most comfortable around people he knew well, and he felt awkward and out of place at social gatherings, particularly those affairs that attracted the rich and powerful. Nixon apparently was deficient in social control—the ability to social role-play. Social control is critical for the charismatic politician, who needs both the emotional loyalty of the masses and the respect of the elite.

Nixon's tendency to shy away from the limelight, the very place where the charismatic leader thrives, was perhaps most apparent in the 1972 presidential campaign. Faced with what was most assuredly his greatest political triumph, Nixon chose to limit severely his personal campaigning. In some ways, Nixon may have felt that his communication deficiencies might have sabotaged his reelection, as the debates with Kennedy had scuttled his 1960 campaign. A truly charismatic leader would have seized the opportunity to strengthen his own position and hold on followers—to exercise the skills that are the master crafts of the charismatic leader.

So far, we have been concentrating primarily on charismatic leaders of political movements. This makes sense, for it is these leaders who have played major roles in shaping political and social history. However, in the world of business and commerce, there are powerful figures—figures also possessing charisma—who have played an important part in shaping the economic growth of nations. For many years, these powerful business leaders have been behind the scenes, using their money and influence to shape political and public policy. However, we are becoming increasingly aware of charismatic leaders of business and industry, as they step out from the shadows and into the public eye—some of them emerging as charismatic candidates for powerful political positions. In the next chapter, we will look at charisma and how it is used to lead productive and powerful work organizations, and we will examine how social skills aid in the ability to get certain jobs done.

✳ 6 ✳

Leadership in the Workplace: The Charismatic Manager

It has been estimated that as much as 80 percent of a typical manager's day is spent communicating. If it is true that the majority of a manager's or supervisor's job involves communication, then it makes perfect sense that the best managers are likely to be those who are the most effective communicators.

Management theorist Henry Mintzberg proposes that managers play many roles.[1] Most of these are directly related to communication. For example, managers serve as *spokespersons* for subordinates, representing the work group to those higher up in the organization and to people outside of the company. The manager also serves as *monitor* and *disseminator* of important work-related information. *Decision-making* roles are also part of the manager's job—choosing courses of action for the work group and settling disputes between subordinates. Finally, the manager serves as a *leader,* motivating workers, advising them, and coordinating activities and operations. All of these managerial activities involve the basic skill components that we have been talking about—expressing oneself verbally and nonverbally, being sensitive to the communications of others, controlling feelings, and playing certain roles effectively. It seems clear that individuals who have well-developed social skills are more likely to be effective managers, and they may become charismatic leaders of work groups.

The most well-known research on leadership in the workplace has found that there are two styles of leadership behavior that are related to managerial success. These are referred to as task-oriented and relationship-oriented behaviors.[2]

Task-oriented leaders are concerned with getting the job done. They assign specific tasks to each subordinate, set standards of work output, and direct activities. Task-oriented leaders emphasize the meeting of deadlines and envision subordinates working together as a unit—like a well-oiled piece of machinery. As you might suspect, task-oriented managers usually have work groups that are productive, but morale may suffer since workers may feel that the task-oriented manager does not care about them as persons.

Relationship-oriented leaders, on the other hand, are concerned with establishing good interpersonal relations with subordinates. They try to set up a work situation in which everyone gets along. Relationship-oriented leaders are genuinely concerned for employees' welfare and for their feelings. They believe that it is important that the company work together like a family. Relationship-oriented managers lead work groups with high morale and loyalty, but production may suffer because the manager may not set concrete goals or may shy away from giving explicit orders to subordinates.

While it may sound as if the two leadership styles are incompatible, near opposites, this is not the case. Managers can possess one, both, or none of the two styles. Although there has been quite a deal of controversy over which leadership style is the best, recent research seems to indicate that managers who have both task- and relationship-oriented leadership styles are the most successful.[3]

If we examine how these two leadership styles are related to the communication skills that underlie charisma, it appears that effective task-oriented leaders make important use of their skills in the social/verbal realm. To be successful, they must be able to give clear written and spoken instructions to subordinates—in other words, they must be socially expressive. Good task-oriented managers must also quickly and easily understand the verbal feedback coming from subordinates and should be able to decipher the orders and messages filtering down from the upper levels of the organization. Skill in social sensitivity is important here. Finally, skill in social control can help the task-oriented manager to play the many decision-making roles associated with his or her position successfully (e.g., serving as ''judge'' of subordinates' disputes or serving as formal spokesperson for the group).

Skills in emotional communication are essential for the success of the relationship-oriented manager. Sincerity and concern for others is communicated most effectively through nonverbal channels. The relationship-oriented manager needs to have emotional empathy. He must be sensitive to the feelings and needs of subordinates and must be able to express true caring for workers and for their concerns. The skills of emotional expressivity and emotional sensitivity are crucial for the relationship-oriented manager.

If we assume that it is best for a manager to possess both task-oriented and relationship-oriented behaviors, then the most important thing he can learn is *when* to be a task-oriented leader and *when* to be relationship-oriented. This involves adjusting his style of behavior to fit the needs of the particular situation. Here again, the basic social skills that we have been discussing are critically important. The socially skilled manager possesses the sensitivity needed to assess a certain work situation. He is attuned to the feelings of subordinates, but also is aware of the various social rules that are in effect—rules governing what is appropriate and inappropriate managerial behavior in each situation.

Secondly, the effective manager must be a master of emotional self-control. A good leader needs to be able to put personal feelings on hold and make objective and fair decisions. Most importantly, skills in the area of control help the socially skilled leader adjust his personal leadership style to fit the situation best.

Finally, the effective business leader must project an image of confidence and competence. As skills in social control are related to feeling socially self-confident, public-speaking skills (social expressivity) are critical to presenting information clearly and directly. If we examine charismatic business leaders, most often we see both task- and person-oriented leadership styles.

Lee Iacocca, head of the Chrysler Corporation and former president of the Ford Motor Company, is a particularly well-known charismatic business leader. While Iacocca has a reputation as a hard-nosed, ``get-the-job-done'' leader, co-workers close to him indicate that he also has tremendous people skills.

> He is a warm, impassioned, and zealous individual . . . Always maintaining of sense of quiet dignity in public, he is nonetheless a witty and charming man.
>
> There's a piece of him that's kind and very, very gentle, a gentleman not only with his family, where he is extraordinary, but with the men he works with.[4]

Iacocca appears to have both the task-oriented and relationship-oriented leadership styles that are characteristic of the most effective managers. Moreover, Lee Iacocca has many of the same qualities that are important in any kind of charismatic leader—he is able to inspire and motivate subordinates, he is an excellent and persuasive public speaker, and he has left a long trail of very successful accomplishments.

> . . . he is an easy leader to follow, an inspiration to do their jobs. He never asks a man to do anything he can't or won't do himself.[5]

Great leaders are made, not born. Charismatic leaders of work groups, political groups, or any other type of following become effective and charismatic through the development of their social skills; they learn to be charismatic, and charisma is often the key to success. Lee

Iacocca, or any other charismatic business leader, can point to the intense learning processes, continual practice, and honing of skills that have led to the development of an effective leadership style.

Anyone possessing well-developed social skills has the basic tools necessary to become an effective and charismatic manager. (And, as we will see later, anybody can develop their social skills and, thus, enhance their charisma potential through practice, dedication, and desire.)

Of course, being an effective manager means more than being just a charismatic communicator. Effective managers are also good decision makers, they are organized, and they are self-motivated. Yet, the social skills underlying charisma may also help in these areas.

Good decision making involves gathering pertinent information on which to base important management decisions. Managers who are effective communicators, and who are "in touch" with co-workers are going to be efficient data gatherers. They are likely to be sensitive to what is going on in the workplace, and they will ask the right questions to get the information they need quickly.[6]

In the same vein, a manager who can clearly and explicitly articulate orders and directions to subordinates, and who demands clear-cut feedback, will usually be the supervisor of an organized department. Socially skilled managers know how to delegate work and are careful to set up a monitoring system to ensure that the work is being done correctly and efficiently. There is a free flow and exchange of ideas and information between the charismatic manager and workers.

Finally, a socially skilled, charismatic manager will usually receive the loyalty and admiration of subordinates. The charismatic manager has a type of influence over subordinates that is called *referent power*.[7] This exists when subordinates obey a manager out of a sense of admiration and liking. Typically, a charismatic leader develops a strong referent power base because he or she is perceived by followers as being sincere and trustworthy. Being emotionally sensitive and expressing true feelings of gratitude (or displeasure) can lead to the impression that the leader is indeed sincere, which can only serve to enhance further the charismatic leader's referent power.

A leader may also use other power bases to become an influential and successful manager. The leader may have control over followers because he is able to reward them. On the other hand, a leader may exercise control by punishing or threatening to punish subordinates. These two power bases are called *reward power* and *coercive power*. The wise leader strives to limit the use of coercive power while trying to maximize rewards for loyal, productive followers. Since coercive power involves the use of punishment—inflicting harm on others—the continual use of coercive power can lead to resentment and anger in those punished, which eventually leads to an eroding of the leader's referent power base.

Leaders may also rule by virtue of some legitimate title or position they hold. Workers will obey the orders of persons who are called "manager," "supervisor," or "vice-president" because of what is called the *legitimate power* base. We are conditioned to follow the directions of those persons who are legitimately in charge.

Finally, a leader may be followed because he possesses some special skill, talent, or knowledge that is important to the group. This last power base is referred to as *expert power*. All of the five power bases are important to effective leaders and managers, but it is possession of high levels of referent power that most clearly distinguishes the charismatic leader from other successful leaders.

The charismatic manager needs to understand the dynamics of the various power bases in order to enhance his influence over followers. Ideally, the different power bases should work together. A truly strong, charismatic leader possesses all of the power bases. The charismatic leader is deeply admired and liked (referent power), has some recognized authority over followers (legitimate power), and possesses true leadership skills (expert power). Also important are the ability to provide for followers' needs (reward power) and a willingness to chastise group members who are guilty of some wrong-doing (coercive power). The power bases can be used wisely by the charismatic leader, for the good of the entire group, or they can be used in a selfish way, benefitting only the leader. We will discuss this further in Chapter 8.

In our research on charisma in the workplace, we have found that successful managers generally tend to possess well-developed social skills. In short, the more socially skilled and charismatic the manager, the more likely it is that he or she is in a position of great re-sponsibility and power.[8] But this does not mean that all charismatic managers look and act in the same way. As we have seen in the "charisma profiles," charismatic persons possess different amounts and balances of the six basic social skills that, when combined, make up charisma. Different types of charismatic, successful man-agers may rely on different social-skill strengths. A com-parison of two charismatic managers from our research will help to illustrate this.

Charles is the director of human resources for a fairly large insurance organization. While Charles pos-sesses high charisma potential, his greatest strength is his expressiveness. Charles is a great talker—a salesman. He has worked himself into an influential position in his present company in a very short time (he held a lower position in a smaller company less than a year ago) through his ability to sell himself, his ideas, and his programs. Charles is emotionally expressive, radiating warmth and positive emotions. Most people instantly take a liking to him. Give him an audience and a topic, and Charles can speak intelligently and entertainingly for half an hour. As a co-worker notes:

> At first you think Charles has come by for a friendly chat, but after a while you realize that he's doing a sales job, trying to get your support for one of his pet projects. But you don't care. He's doing it in such a friendly, persuasive way that you *want* to back him . . . Chuck could sell anything to anybody.

Paula is also a charismatic manager, but in a very different way.

A vice-president in charge of cost accounting for an electronics manufacturing firm, Paula's social-skill strengths are in the areas of social sensitivity and emotional and social control. Paula radiates confidence. She looks like a person who is completely ''in charge.'' Formal, yet polite, Paula is always said to be fair, but firm, in her dealings with subordinates. As Paula's company president told me:

> Paula's the one we turn to in a crisis—difficult negotiations, when we need a ''knock-em-dead'' presentation . . . She's probably the most trusted person in the entire company.

In contrast to Charles, Paula relies less on overt expressiveness to influence others. She uses her social skills to project a certain role—that of a confident and capable administrator and leader. She is very studied and controlled in her interactions, relying more on objective analysis of situations than on appealing to the emotions of others (Charles's forte). Although different in behavioral styles, both Paula and Charles are highly socially skilled, and both are charismatic (as rated by co-workers, and from scores on the SSI). Since charisma is composed of several basic social skills, specific strengths in one or more of these can lead to different forms of charisma.

CHARISMA PROFILES: MANAGERS CHARLES AND PAULA

To illustrate how different strengths in the various basic social skills can lead to very different types of charismatic personalities, we will compare the profiles of the two charismatic managers, Charles and Paula.

As you remember, Charles's strengths were his expressive skills. He appears to have a high energy level due to his emotional and verbal expressiveness. Charles is less strong in sensitivity skills (although still above average), which means he is more of a "talker" than a "listener." Entrepreneur Ted Turner, head of WTBS and owner of the Atlanta Braves, is a similar type of charismatic manager—expressive with "salesmanship" skills.

Paula, on the other hand, relies on her strengths in the areas of emotional and social control (yet she shows a good balance of all of the basic social skills). Her confident, "in-control" style of dealing with others leads to a very different type of charismatic profile, one of being serious, but open and fair. Paula's profile might be similar to that of Chrysler's Lee Iacocca.

So far, this discussion has dealt primarily with charisma as a key to being an effective manager, but pos-

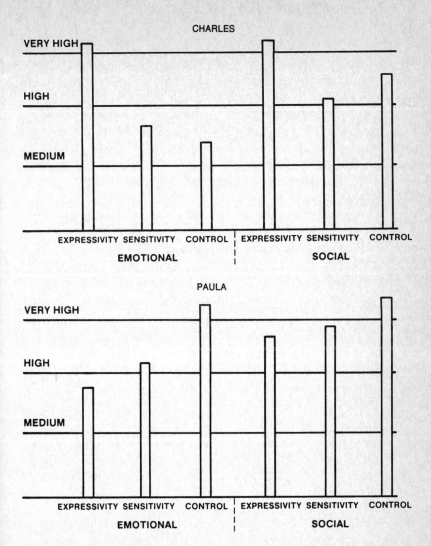

CHARLES

VERY HIGH

HIGH

MEDIUM

EXPRESSIVITY SENSITIVITY   CONTROL | EXPRESSIVITY SENSITIVITY   CONTROL

EMOTIONAL   SOCIAL

PAULA

VERY HIGH

HIGH

MEDIUM

EXPRESSIVITY SENSITIVITY   CONTROL | EXPRESSIVITY SENSITIVITY   CONTROL

EMOTIONAL   SOCIAL

session of charisma can be beneficial to a variety of
professions where communication is an integral part of
the job. Persons involved in public-relations work, customer service, teaching, and the helping professions (so-

cial work, nursing, etc.) can greatly improve their abilities to do their jobs by developing their social skills and charisma potential. Of course, certain types of jobs rely more heavily on certain dimensions of social skill. For example, salespersons rely strongly on expressive skills to aid in making good sales presentations. Effective counselors need to be sensitive to what the client is saying, both at the verbal and the emotional level. Effective judges need to have skills in emotional and social control in order to detach themselves from their own feelings about a case, and to help present images of fairness and impartiality. Communication skills and charisma are very important in a wide variety of jobs, particularly jobs that involve dealing with other people.

Perhaps the professions where charisma and social skills are of the greatest importance are in those occupations that deal solely with communications. Persons employed in the various communication media, particularly those individuals who appear before us on movie and television screens, must be exceptionally skilled communicators. We will examine the role of charisma in the media next.

❊ 7 ❊

Charisma and the Media

From the earliest beginnings of civilization, there have no doubt been charismatic individuals—socially skilled persons who have used their influence over others to achieve great deeds. For the most part, their communicative powers were exercised primarily through personal contacts. Yet, in the twentieth century, the mass media—newspaper, film, radio, and television—have instantly brought charismatic individuals directly to the eyes and ears of millions. Today, the media is used to extend the reach of charismatic figures.

CHARISMA AND MEDIA POLITICS

World leaders appear on a daily basis before their followers in morning newspaper photos and articles and on nightly television news programs. Snatches of the latest speech are broadcast hourly over radio news networks. Through the use of the media, the modern leader can keep in constant touch with supporters and can quickly call them to action.

While all contemporary leaders make use of mass media, it is the charismatic leader who is most likely to be aware of their potential and to use the media to their fullest extent. It is interesting to note that famous historical charismatic leaders seem instantly to recognize the value of media technology and hasten to put it to use. President Theodore Roosevelt was a pioneer in seeing the political potential of motion pictures. Throughout his various campaigns and expeditions, Roosevelt's exploits were recorded by a film crew. During the Second World War, Winston Churchill and Franklin Roosevelt made constant use of the radio, both to comfort and reassure their respective citizenry, and to garner support for the war effort. Following his triumphant televised debates with Nixon, John Kennedy became convinced of the power of television to reach all corners of the nation, and he made extensive use of the medium throughout his presidency. Ronald Reagan, a former actor, is an expert at using the media. His experience in films and television has led to the creation of a confident and comfortable image on the television screen that has seemed to work well in attracting popular support. In fact, Reagan may be the most effective ``visual'' President in U.S. history.

Theodore H. White, who has chronicled U.S. presidential campaigns in his series of books on *The Making of the President,* states that the media, and television in particular, have revolutionized how our leaders are chosen. Surveys indicate that the majority of the U.S. population receives news about the world, and information about world leaders, from television. The successful candidate for political office must carefully consider how he or she appears to the television-viewing public. Careful cultivation of the candidate's television image is imperative.

> Every waking day, the average American family has its television set flickering for more or less five hours; and as much additional time is spent listening to radio. The purpose of a campaign now is to capture as much of this audience as possible . . . Television has made the personality of the candidate central; his quirks, hair style, skin color, voice tone, and apparent sincerity are as important as his themes and programs.[1]

The late 1970s and early 1980s saw the overwhelming impact of television in leader selection. Although there is no general agreement as to former President Jimmy Carter's possession of charisma, Carter was a skilled communicator, an experienced politician, and perhaps most important, a quick learner. His opponent in the 1976 presidential campaign, Gerald Ford, did not come across as well visually—very important in the usual television format. Although Ford and Carter each hired a force of television consultants, strategists, and ''image-makers,'' the Carter team seemed to have the edge and eventually came away with the victory. The expertise of Carter's television advisers notwithstanding, Carter's ability to form a better television persona was probably the true key to his success.

Carter learned television fast. His smile went on as soon as the camera's red light flashed, as if he were plugged in. If the organization, run by Hamilton Jordan, could provide the (primary) victories, Carter could stretch those victories, by television, into more and yet more victories . . . No candidate had used television better than Jimmy Carter up to 1976.[2]

The basic social skills of expressivity and control are central to a candidate's ability to come across well on television. An ability to express oneself verbally (social expressivity), is perhaps the most important skill a political candidate can possess. But television is a visual medium. To be seen as sincere and honest, skills in emotional expressivity are also required. (If sincerity is to be feigned, then being a gifted emotional actor—skill in emotional control—will serve the candidate well.) In certain situations, the wily politician may choose to express some emotional message to arouse the sympathy of the audience (e.g., Nixon's "Checkers" speech), or to whip up some supporter enthusiasm for the long campaign battle ahead. At times, a leader may show a flash of anger, accompanied by an indignant reaction, displaying that the leader is a take-charge kind of person. Author White illustrates just such a case during the 1980 presidential campaign as Ronald Reagan, George Bush, and other Republican presidential hopefuls were about to meet for a debate in a New England high school gymnasium.

The cameras begin to roll . . . Then follows what could not have been more than ninety seconds of drama. Ronald Reagan reaches for the microphone to explain the tableau. Mr. Breen (the debate moderator) snaps aloud to the technicians: "Turn Mr. Reagan's microphone off." Then Reagan jackknifes up from his chair, grabs the microphone in a single swoop, his temper flaring, and yells, "I paid for this show. I'm paying for this microphone, Mr. Green [sic]."

The swoop, the grace, the perfect flow of the dramatic gesture could not have been better if rehearsed a dozen times. Here was an indignant citizen defending his rights; the outraged motorist taking no lip from the motorcycle cop; the workingman talking back to management. The audience of working-class youngsters cheered. . . .

The rest of the debate was a closet drama of no great significance . . . But the cameras had had their snatch of reality: Ronald Reagan's outburst of vivid yet controlled emotion . . . The next day . . . New England and national television were to fill the news void with ninety seconds of Reagan's insurrection against the authorities . . . Not until forty-eight hours later, watching television, did I realize that Ronald Reagan had won the Republican nomination, hands down, right there.[3]

Ronald Reagan, the former motion-picture actor, is also the consummate political actor. It is the basic skill of social control that underlies his ability to play roles. Persons possessing social control also convey an aura of self-confidence, derived from faith in their ability to handle just about any social situation, that makes socially controlled persons very appealing to others. Much of our research on basic social skills supports this notion that socially controlled persons are evaluated favorably.[4] Persons high in social control may also be seen as more honest and trustworthy. While it appears that the ability to display controlled emotions (such as Reagan's outburst during the New England debates) and the skill of social control are two elements that make up Reagan's tremendous charismatic appeal, there is another key ingredient.

I stumbled on this key component of Reagan's charisma quite by accident. In 1980, at the time of the 1980 presidential campaign, I was teaching a course in nonverbal communication. Each student in the course had been assigned a class presentation on an area of communication. One student chose the Carter-Reagan debates as his topic. He decided to try to replicate a finding that was widely reported during the 1960 Kennedy-Nixon debates, that persons watching the 1960 debates on television were seemingly impressed by Kennedy's youthful, charismatic presence and felt that Kennedy had "won" the debates. People listening to the debates on the radio were likely to give the edge to Nixon.[5]

The student's attempts to replicate these results with the Carter-Reagan debates were inconclusive. But while he was making his presentation, accompanied by a videotaped portion of the debates, he would occasionally pause the videotape, usually freezing one of the candidates' faces on the screen. As the student would pause and then restart the videotape, I began to notice a clear difference in the facial expressions of Reagan and Carter. Carter's expressions were fairly consistent, either very neutral or serious-looking with an occasional positive, smiling face. Reagan's facial expressions were much more diverse and constantly changing. The tape would pause with Reagan frozen in mid-statement. His eyes were open wide, eyebrows arched, with mouth agape—as if surprised. Yet, when the tape was restarted, the statement contained nothing that would cause him to be surprised. When paused again, Reagan's face would display anger or rage, but his statement and tone of voice would be free from any indication of anger. At another time, the expression would be sad, then fearful. With the videotape running at its normal speed, it was impossible to detect these subtle changes in Reagan's expressions.

I concluded that Reagan was simply more emotionally animated than Carter. As Reagan spoke, his expressions were in constant flux, as he "colored" his speech with fleeting emotional displays. I began to call the tendency to display these continuous, momentary expressions *emotional lability.* In studies since this time, we have found that people vary quite a bit in their emotional lability. Generally, charismatic persons tend to be more emotionally labile than noncharismatic persons, although this is not always the case.[6]

It seems that this emotional lability is one of the components of dynamic attractiveness, for our subsequent research has found that people who display more of this facial animation make more positive impressions on others in initial encounters. Emotional lability also seems to be linked to skill in emotional expressivity. Thus, it is Reagan's combination of controlled acting ability, leading to a projection of self-confidence, and the extraordinary emotional feeling that he puts into his messages, that contribute to his special, and very powerful, type of charismatic appeal—a certain type of charisma that comes across very well on television.[7]

Today's leaders need to be more and more concerned with their visual image. In this era ruled by mass media, charismatic leaders may have more powerful appeal than at any other time in history. Yet, charisma involves more than just visual appeal. Truly charismatic persons are socially skilled in a variety of ways. It is interesting to note that many famous charismatic leaders are exceptionally skilled verbal and written communicators. The majority of historical charismatic political leaders have been accomplished and renowned authors. Winston Churchill was a prolific and critically acclaimed journalist before the age of thirty. John F. Kennedy won the Pulitzer Prize for his book, *Profiles in Courage.* Theodore, Franklin Delano, and Eleanor Roosevelt were all recognized for various contributions to literature. And the political and philosphical writings of Gandhi, Mao Tse Tung, and Martin Luther King, Jr., have been read by millions.

Charismatic leadership and the various written, visual, and spoken media are naturally linked. Newspapers, television, and radio all mix well with modern politics. Today's charismatic politicians are true media figures. But the various media have also introduced us to charismatic figures who are not political leaders—persons who put themselves on display and use their various social skills solely to entertain.

CHARISMA AND THE SILVER SCREEN

Motion-picture actors and actresses comprise a large portion of our modern-day charismatic figures. By virtue of their profession, they are bound to develop many basic social skills. They spend years perfecting role-playing skills (social control), they learn to portray various emotions on cue (emotional expressivity and emotional control), and they are trained to react to the behaviors of fellow actors (social and emotional sensitivity).

When we have asked people to list charismatic persons, our respondents typically include two or more film stars. Aside from the developed social skills possessed by actors and actresses, there are other reasons why many film stars are commonly seen as charismatic.

First and foremost, film stars are among the most media-exposed (overexposed?) persons in the world. A hit motion picture exposes its stars to an audience of millions in the space of a few weeks. The presence of film stars in movie tabloids, on television talk shows and variety shows, and in older movies rerun at all hours on television, insures that movie stars are constantly in the public eye. Importantly, people throughout the world seem fascinated with the movies and with movie stars, and seem unable to get enough of them. Film stars are idolized and emulated.

More than just the fact that movie stars receive tremendous amounts of media exposure, a number of psychological factors also come into play. Movie stars' presence on the big screen means that they are presented to us as literally ''larger than life.'' Many successful film stars live in huge, protected estates. Their wealth and status mean that they can go places and attend events from which the rest of us are excluded. Moreover, the images and physical persons of major film stars are carefully protected. They are isolated from, and elevated above, the common population.

Most typically, charismatic film stars play heroic roles. (It is rare that an actor or actress will attain charismatic status by playing primarily villainous roles.) In their film roles, the heroes are usually successful—they win the battle, get the girl, and on the rare occasions that they die, usually go out in a blaze of glory. It is no small wonder then that the general public reveres and idolizes their film stars. They appear as persons of monumental status and importance, are incredibly successful, and possess coveted talents. Because we look up to charismatic movie stars, they, too, possess the ability to influence us in the same way as charismatic political leaders.

Advertisers have considerable faith in the charisma of stars. Film stars are paid enormous sums of money to endorse products. Companies believe that charismatic actors and actresses will be able to inspire the masses to buy their products. To some extent, this strategy may be quite successful.

The film stars who are most likely to be labeled charismatic are usually those who incorporate bits of themselves into the roles they play. Aspects of the performers' true personalities remain and are exhibited in spite of their roles. Robert Redford, Clint Eastwood, Shirley MacLaine, and Paul Newman are film stars who have been frequently mentioned as charismatic in our latest surveys of the public. These stars, particularly Robert Redford and Clint Eastwood, retain something of themselves in each role that they play.

Character actors, or stars who change their behavior and appearance greatly from role to role, are less likely to be mentioned as charismatic. Sir Laurence Olivier and Robert DeNiro take great pains to hide their true personalities, and even their true physical appearance, in an effort to ``become'' the role. Both Olivier and DeNiro are included less frequently in lists of charismatic film stars. However, it is important to keep in mind that nearly all famous actors are likely to possess the basic social skills that determine charisma potential. Indeed, our research has shown that social skills and acting experience are correlated.[8] Experienced actors and actresses tend to possess more of the basic social skills underlying charisma. Yet, we do not know whether these persons develop their extraordinary social skills through acting and in acting classes, or if people with exceptional social skills are drawn into acting as a career. In all probability, both are true.

Perhaps nothing more dramatically demonstrates the impact of acting skills than the election of Ronald Reagan as President. Reagan's acting expertise came in quite handy in the making of televised campaign commercials.

He was able to make quick and thoroughly professional commercials for each region of the country in which he was campaigning. These commercials would address timely, local issues, enhancing the public's perception that candidate Reagan was in touch with their specific concerns. No doubt, Reagan's professional acting experience gave him the edge over amateur actors Jimmy Carter and Walter Mondale when it came to campaigning through the media.

CHARISMA AND TELEVISION

Television, as opposed to films, is a more informal medium. Whereas the film screen is large and imposing, the television screen is small and personal. Television comes into our homes and is incorporated into our daily lives. Movie stars become charismatic by impressing us on the grand scale. Television personalities who are labeled charismatic seem to draw our attention and admiration through their extraordinary ``people skills.'' The most commonly mentioned charismatic television stars include Johnny Carson, Bill Cosby, Carol Burnett, Phil Donahue, and Alan Alda.[9]

Carson and Donahue are among television's finest interviewers. Each has an ability to establish rapport with an audience. Each has a devoted following of loyal viewers. Both Carson and Donahue (along with Cosby, Burnett, and Alda) come across as sensitive, caring human beings. They seem to be the kinds of people the public would like to get to know on a personal basis. Television personalities also appear on a regular basis, keeping them in weekly or daily contact with the viewing public. The charismatic influence of television stars, as opposed to film stars, is likely to be a more intimate or personal bond with viewers.

A new group of television celebrities who are beginning to take on charismatic qualities are television news anchorpersons. In the early days of TV news broadcasting, the news reporter was little more than a "talking head"—news reports were read in a clear, but emotionless, voice, with little real interaction between the news anchorperson and the other news reporters. In fact, the words that they spoke were not even their own, but were written by a team of newswriters, and read from a script or teleprompter.

Today's news anchorperson is still expected to be objective in reporting the news, but emotionality is no longer banned. The anchorperson is allowed to display some emotional sympathy in the wake of a tragedy, or glimmers of positive emotions in response to some happy news item. The anchorperson now also engages in good-natured banter with other news reporters and conducts interviews of field reporters, eyewitnesses, and special guests. In short, the communication skills required of the anchorperson now go beyond simple ability to express oneself verbally.

The gifted anchorperson needs to be able to display subtle, yet controlled, emotions. He or she needs to be a sensitive, yet probing, interviewer. The anchorperson must have human qualities—knowing how to tell a joke and how to take one. He or she must maintain an attractive image and exude self-confidence and honesty. The anchorperson also needs to be able to get along with the rest of the members of the news team, must be a leader and a coordinator of their activities. Today's more well-rounded, socially skilled television news anchorpersons thus become candidates for charismatic status, unlike the unidimensional newspersons of yesteryear.

Names such as Jane Pauley, Peter Jennings, and Tom Brokaw now appear regularly on lists of charismatic persons. TV news anchorpersons are admired, respected, and most importantly, greatly trusted by their loyal viewers.

CHARISMA, TV, AND RELIGION: THE MEDIATED MINISTRY[10]

Perhaps no group of leaders relies so heavily on charismatic powers as do leaders of religious groups. In fact, throughout history, charisma has often been viewed as being divinely inspired.*

Charismatic religious leaders were quick to realize the potential power of the media to reach the unconfirmed masses. The charismatic power certain preachers displayed in churches and in tent revival meetings transferred well to the airwaves. Religious radio programs began broadcasting in the 1920s. Among the more famous of these media pioneers was the charismatic Roman Catholic bishop, Fulton J. Sheen. Sheen began broadcasting sermons over the radio in 1928 and made the successful transition to television in the 1950s.

> Sheen was able to sustain the interest of and communicate to a wide range of people of all faiths . . . Interest in the program was sustained solely by Sheen's meticulous planning, vocal variety, facial expressions, ges-

*It is important to note here that we are discussing charisma from a "personality" perspective. In our discussion of the charisma of religious leaders, we are referring to personal charisma possessed by the leader, not to the so-called "charismatic" religious movement.

tures, the relevance of his content, and the dynamic of his authoritative personality.[11]

Today, the television ministry has greatly expanded. TV preachers reach a wide and far-ranging audience, and they have tremendous influence over their congregations, as evidenced by the size of the monetary contributions they receive. Among the more well-known charismatic leaders of religious programs are Oral Roberts, Robert Schuller, and Jerry Falwell. Each of these religious leaders, and dozens of others, have built their television ministries into powerful and influential forces affecting millions. The main factor related to these TV ministers success lies in their charisma—their extraordinary abilities to communicate. To be charismatic, and to have impact on viewers, television preachers must be expressive, clearly articulating the Word and imbuing the message with emotional life. It is essential that viewers' feel this emotional or ''spiritual'' uplift. (Remember the process of emotional contagion we discussed earlier?) Television evangelists also need to be sensitive to the needs and meet the expectations of their viewers. The minister must also have a sense of ''presence''—a controlled and confident air that inspires faith from the congregation. Again, the basic skills of expressivity, sensitivity, and control underly these communicative powers possessed by the successful TV minister. Of course, charisma alone is not going to turn a preacher into a multimillion-dollar religious organization, as Peter Horsfield notes in his book, *Religious Television:*

> There is a strong charisma in these men which separates them from the thousands of other faithful preachers . . . But their charisma alone has not produced these success stories. Their success is also a result of a careful and

determined marketing: the product of a unique blending of charisma with personal drive and audacity, accurate social intuition, hard-nosed business advice and judgment, and adoption of modern marketing principles and techniques.[12]

The power of charismatic television evangelists should not be underestimated. Television ministers are more than an Oral Roberts inspiring a congregation with words and music, or a Reverend Schuller holding an audience spellbound with a dramatic sermon. Religion, morality, social values, and politics are all conveyed by these charismatic TV personalities. The rise of Jerry Falwell's Moral Majority, and the impact it had in the 1980 election outcome, indicate that the power of these charismatic figures extends far beyond simple Sunday services in an entertaining, televised format.[13] Indeed, Pat Robertson, one of the TV preachers, has announced his candidacy for the 1988 U.S. presidential election.

CHARISMA AND MIXED MEDIA: MUSIC, MOVIES, AND MTV[14]

There is a tendency for some people to equate charisma with popularity. Persons are assumed to possess charisma in direct proportion to how much attention they receive from the public. This is not the case. Individuals can become popular for a specific achievement, or for some special talent, yet they can be lacking the social skills that are required for charisma. Nowhere is this more clearly demonstrated than in the field of popular music.

Throughout the twentieth century, popular singers, songwriters, and musicians have received the acclaim and adoration of the public, who buy their records and attend their concerts by the millions. In spite of their popularity, musical superstars are only rarely mentioned on lists of famous charismatic persons (in spite of the fact that many of the lists are generated by those mass consumers of popular music, college students). There are several reasons for this.

First, although music is a form of communication, it is not the same type of face-to-face communication used in political speeches or religious sermons. Musicians create certain sounds that are pleasing and that often convey feeling, but they are of a more general, rather than personal, nature. It is the message—the music itself—that has much of the appeal to the listener, rather than the person creating the message. The music, in a way, becomes disassociated from the performer.

Secondly, the musician uses the music to make statements to the audience in the same way that an artist might use a painting to communicate a message. Therefore, the talents of musicians (and artists) are invested in the creation. It takes on a communicative life of its own. The artwork itself speaks to the audience. Thus, it is unlikely that the typical musician will give much attention to developing the interpersonal communication skills that are central to charisma.

Finally, music has been primarily an auditory medium. Unless attending a live performance (and getting a good enough seat actually to be able to see the performer), the audience only hears the musical performer; and we know how important visuals are to charisma. Until recently, pop stars rarely appeared on television or in films. And, when they did appear, it was usually a pantomimed, ``lip-sync'' performance rather than a live presentation of a musical number. Since the audience has only seen a limited side of most popular music stars, it is not surprising that very few musicians are labeled charismatic.

In the past, on those rare occasions when a music star did get a chance to display some non–music communication skills, through a role in a film or on a television show, they more often than not were unprepared and/or displayed poor natural acting skills. Two notable early exceptions from years gone by were Frank Sinatra and Bing Crosby. Although neither was a spectacular, award-winning actor, each had creditable performances in several motion pictures, and both have achieved some charismatic status, perhaps as much through their film and television appearances as their musical performances. More recent musicians who are becoming candidates for charismatic status via film roles are David Bowie, Bette Midler, and Sting.

While pop music superstars used to appear only sporadically on TV and in films, it is becoming a much more common occurrence, particularly with the introduction of music videos—the merging of recorded music and visual performances. With the introduction of entire shows, and even an entire television channel, devoted solely to exposing music performers to the TV-viewing public, we should expect many future charismatic personalities to emerge from the music world.

We have seen how the media play an important part in bringing socially skilled, charismatic figures to the masses, increasing the power and influence of these charismatic persons. The media, particularly television, can instantly unleash charisma potential. But in the same way, the media can quickly reveal an individual who has deficits in basic communication skills. While the media has "made" charismatic superstars, it also exposes those who are less gifted.

In the 1972 Olympics, U.S. swimmer Mark Spitz won an unprecedented seven gold medals. As soon as the games were over, Spitz was inundated with hundreds of offers including guest appearances on television shows, newspaper and magazine interviews, endorsement of products, and movie contracts. Everyone expected the handsome Spitz to become a superstar, grossing millions and millions of dollars. However, his guest appearances on a Bob Hope television special and on *The Bill Cosby Show* in the fall of 1972 received terrible reviews. Critics called Spitz "a fish out of water" and pronounced him devoid of acting talent. The offers quickly slowed, and Mark Spitz never became the superstar many had predicted.

Spitz probably possessed average levels of communication skills, but he had no particular acting expertise and little knowledge about handling the media. All of the post-Olympic hype led to tremendous expectations. People expected Mark Spitz to be a charismatic media figure. However, the public was greatly disappointed in his amateurish television acting debut. Since that time, Spitz has become a reasonably good sports commentator, but he never achieved any spectacular success, most likely because he lacked certain basic components of charisma potential.

Thus, we see that the media is a powerful tool that can launch an individual into the public eye in an instant. However, charisma itself lies in the individual. The media cannot "make" a person charismatic, unless he or she already possesses the basic potential.

We know that charisma can be a powerful force to influence others. And we have seen how the media can be used to extend and enhance the appeal of certain charismatic figures. Yet, the use of charismatic power is not always benign. Charisma can be used for positive ends, but is can also be used for evil purposes, as we shall see in the next chapter.

✳ 8 ✳

Charisma for Good and for Evil

My own opinion is that he was a genius and that he might have done much good . . . had he not given way to demoniacal forces[1]

—Heinz Assmann on Adolf Hitler

How lucky for the world that Martin Luther King, Jr. was so good a man . . . had he an evil intent, he could have caused more destruction than the most powerful demagogues of our time.[2]

—C. S. King

In the year 1941, the orders of two powerful national leaders were being carried out. In both countries, children were simultaneously being herded into train cars. Both groups were in the process of being "relocated." In one country, the charismatic prime minister, Winston Churchill, was ordering children moved from the city of London to homes in the rural countryside for their own protection, because massive air-raid bombings came nightly to the beleaguered capital city. In the other country, by orders of Der Führer, Adolph Hitler, Jewish children were being loaded into cattle cars, their destination—death camps where they would be systematically murdered.

In 1978, a charismatic American religious leader, Billy Graham, faces a gathering of thousands in an open-air stadium. He exhorts the people to "come forward and pledge your lives to Jesus Chirst." Hundreds of feet instantly respond as potential converts stream to the preacher's platform. At the same time, thousands of miles away in Guyana, another American religious leader calls his congregation forward. This preacher also asks for a pledge of lives. Urged on by the words of the Reverend Jim Jones, the members move forward to drink cyanide-laced punch, lay down, and die.

The powers of charisma can be used for good or for evil. While we most typically think of heroic charismatic individuals leading groups to achieve great deeds, history also tells us of the horror of a tyrannical leader using the power of charisma to enslave followers, forcing them, against their will, to commit atrocious crimes against human nature. Both types of leaders use the power of charisma, but they use it for different ends.

A charismatic leader has the ability to rouse followers to action, and that action may be defined as either morally good or bad. But the distinction is not always clear cut. In wartime, two armies oppose each other. The leader of one army may try to inspire his soldiers to fight by calling on them to destroy the enemy invaders. The other army's general makes a plea to fight for the cause of freedom. Each army then takes the battlefield to kill members of the opposing force, with both leaders feeling as if they, and their men, are morally good. They all believe they are fighting for a just cause. Yet, human lives are being destroyed, the very act of which is usually associated with evil. The lines separating good and evil are very fuzzy. "Good" and "bad" are simply not objective concepts. This moral dilemma presents a particular problem when we talk about the use of charismatic power. For it was, in part, the charisma of Hitler that led to the deaths of millions of innocent persons; and it was the charisma of such men as Franklin Roosevelt and Winston Churchill that helped prevent additional human slaughter.

CHARISMA PROFILE: WINSTON CHURCHILL

British Prime Minister Winston Churchill was one of the great charismatic leaders of the twentieth century. Churchill's greatest social skill strengths were in the areas of social expressivity and social control.

Churchill was an eloquent speaker. Even his political foes were impressed with his verbal skills.

Here was this striking figure in our public life, this sparkling orator . . . his resolution, his marshalling of the facts and his industry, elevated him above his fellows, most of whom were political midgets in comparison.[3]

Throughout the perils of the Second World War, Churchill's public self was an image of strength—one that inspired courage and confidence. Yet, Churchill's charisma profile indicates that he also had skills in the realm of emotional communication. He was compassionate, easily moved by the plight of the common and downtrodden. He also displayed great skill in informal communication. Much of his political strength lay in his ability to form personal ties with the leaders of the other Allied nations.

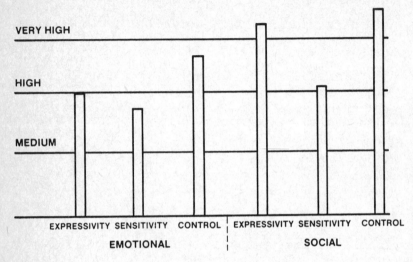

CHARISMA PROFILE: ADOLPH HITLER

The charisma of Adolph Hilter lay primarily in his expressive skills. Not only was Hitler a forceful and rousing speaker, but in face-to-face discussions, he would verbally overwhelm opponents.

Hitler has a method of impressing foreigners and strangers and preventing them from bringing up any issues. He immediately took control of the conversation, kept the floor uninterruptedly, and talked so long and vehemently, that the interview was over before the visitor had a chance to reply—if he had any desire left to do so.[4]

The weak points in Hitler's basic social-skill profile indicate not so much *deficits* in the areas of emotional sensitivity and emotional control, as an inappropriate use of these basic skills. For example, Hitler was reported to have strongly opposed inhumane treatment of animals, yet he displayed unbelievable callousness to the human victims of his political doctrine. Similarly, during his famous deception of Chamberlain (see p. 43), he maintained high emotional control, while, in other instances, he was given to fits of uncontrollable rage.

Hitler, unlike many of the other charismatic figures outlined in this book, showed overall high charisma potential, but much of this was due to his extraordinary expressive skills. Aside from these areas, Hitler's other skill levels were average, and, in some instances, slightly below average. He was not a well-rounded charismatic personality such as a Churchill or Kennedy.

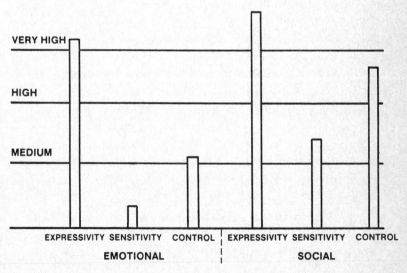

CHARISMA AND
SOCIAL INFLUENCE

All human beings follow certain social rules that govern all forms of social behavior. We take turns when speaking to avoid confusion. We drive only on one side of the road to avoid collisions. When someone asks us a question, we usually answer to be polite. We wear typical kinds of clothing and engage in acceptable types of activities to avoid the criticism of others and subsequent embarrassment. There are thousands of these social rules that serve to make social life flow smoothly.

In his book, *Influence*, social psychologist Robert Cialdini outlines several of the more powerful social rules.[5] Knowledge of how these rules work, and a willingness to put the rules into action, can lead to the powerful ability to influence people, getting them to behave in desired ways. While these social rules can be used by anyone, charismatic persons are most likely to have knowledge of them (due to their high levels of social sensitivity), and they are most likely to be able to put them to use (skills in social expressivity and social control are important here). These social rules can be used by anyone, but when such rules are invoked by powerful charismatic leaders, the results are dramatic and memorable.

Successful charismatic leaders do not rely solely on their skills to inspire followers emotionally, for they know that the loyalty of followers can be fickle. Charismatic leaders also call into play many powerful social processes—using these tactics of influence and manipulation—to attract followers, to keep them in line, and to assure followers' dedication to the cause.

Many times when a leader uses these social rules to influence followers, he or she is treading a thin line between morally good and bad actions. In some cases, the followers may be totally unaware of what the leader is doing. In a sense, these people are being influenced against their better judgment. Some might condemn such leader behavior. On the other hand, it might be argued that people are ultimately responsible for their own actions. The difficulty usually arises when a leader uses charisma and social influence not for good, but for evil, ends.

Good or bad, right or wrong, charismatic leaders throughout history have used influence techniques and strategies to gain their leadership positions and to maintain their powerful hold on followers. What are some of the tactics charismatic leaders use to influence followers?

Careful *impression management* is one way that charismatic leaders attempt to win the support and confidence of followers. We have already seen how important physical appearance is in forming impressions. Charismatic persons, and charismatic leaders in particular, are greatly concerned with their "image." They realize the importance of creating favorable impressions. Leaders need to project an image of strength, confidence, and honesty. And such an image can play an important part in attracting and influencing followers. Our research has shown that skills in social control and expressiveness are very important in the area of impression management.

Historically, charismatic leaders have taken great pains to hide any physical deformities or abnormalities that might indicate signs of weakness. Franklin D. Roosevelt, a victim of polio, took care to see that photographs of his withered legs and braces were not made public. Many of the official pictures of John Kennedy showed him involved in vigorous physical activity, when in reality he had a crippling back injury that severely restricted his movements. Similarly, Adolf Hitler was a small, unimposing, and very ordinary-looking man. Yet, his appearance to the German people was carefully controlled. The image that Hitler was trying to create was that of an imposing, and perhaps invincible, leader. The real Hitler, and the Hitler that the public saw, were very different men.

> Millions of posters, posted in every conceivable place . . . show the Fuehrer as a fairly good-looking individual with a very determined attitude. In addition, the press, newsreels, and so forth, are continually flooded with carefully prepared photographs showing Hitler at his very best.[6]

In the same way that charismatic leaders carefully manage physical appearance, leaders are also careful to manage their ideological selves, putting forth attitudes and values consistent with the positive images they are trying to maintain with the public.

Normally, there is nothing wrong with impression management. Everybody wants to put his or her best face forward. A moral problem arises, however, when an individual blatantly misrepresents himself. Charismatic individuals, skilled in social role-playing, may be particularly adept at being two-faced, presenting one kind of image to people in order to gain their support while hiding true feelings or attitudes. For example, Eva Peron claiming solidarity with the Argentinian poor—her ``shirtless ones''—while secretly living a life of extravagance and amassing a personal fortune at their expense. Adolf Hitler was presented as a true humanitarian, a lover of children and animals, while carrying on a ruthless program of genocide. Rules of impression management are utilized constantly by charismatic leaders.

While careful impression management is the first tactic of social influence often used by charismatic leaders, a second social rule that can be used successfully in influencing others is called the *rule of reciprocity*. People generally strongly believe that one good turn deserves another. In his book, Cialdini makes it clear that this reciprocity rule is very powerful. When we feel as if someone has done something for us, we incur a state of social indebtedness. We want to return the favor. On its surface, this seems to be a just rule. However, in politics and in our judiciary system, there are laws regulating reciprocal arrangements. Politicians and legal officials are not supposed to receive gifts from the public, except under very tightly controlled circumstances. Accusations of bribery and indiscretion may follow a politician's acceptance of a gift, for it is assumed that the politician will later be asked by the gift-giver to return the favor. Of course, many of these systems operate on a double standard. Blatant attempts to influence political officials, through bribes, for example, are frowned upon, while "back-room" reciprocal agreements among politicians are considered to be an acceptable part of the game.

Wise charismatic politicians and religious leaders often invoke the rule of reciprocity when trying to attract followers. A political leader may make promises to improve the economy and raise the standard of living or vow to eliminate crime and make the streets safe to walk again. In return, he or she expects to receive votes and support. Incumbent politicians have an advantage in being able to refer to past accomplishments, pointing to their past deeds as evidence of how they have worked unselfishly for the public good. Religious leaders and groups may offer potential converts eternal salvation in exchange for support. More directly, certain religious groups have begun offering visitors a free meal or gift. Of course, once the prospective member has eaten the meal or accepted the gift, a state of social indebtedness has occurred that now makes the individual more inclined to pay back the group's generosity with personal support.

Jim Jones gained control over members of his People's Temple using the reciprocity rule in an obviously deceptive way. Jones would use his "divine powers" to "heal" members or to save them from physical harm. A first-hand account from 1969 describes a typical Jim Jones service:

> He talked about the current political problems, the war in Vietnam, which he claimed to have prophesied, the government-supported drug racketeering in our country, the social injustices committed against the minorities, the religious hypocrisy in every church but his, and then he finally got around to telling the audience the secret he had been hinting at throughout his sermon.
>
> "I have seen by divine revelation the total annihilation of this country and many other parts of the world . . . The only survivors will be those people who are hiding in a cave that I have been shown in a vision . . ."
>
> He was the first person I had heard who seemed to have a method of salvation from the bomb that I had been fearing for about twenty years. I still didn't want to join his church but I thought I would put our names on his mailing list. Jim promised that the people who were on this list would be notified in two weeks in advance of the actual bomb attack so they could join his members in the cave.

Jones would also claim to have healed Temple members from a variety of tumors and illnesses, and on occasion, he would make prophesies that supposedly would save followers from death or great physical harm.

> ". . . I am being shown that tomorrow morning at about seven thirty when you would have been leaving for work, you would have had an accident and died, but since you came here today you will not have an accident. You will live!" Jim dramatically took a small red cloth from his pulpit and held it out in front of him. "Take this red cloth and wear it on your body for the rest of this month and you will be relieved of that pain you have been suffering in your side."[7]

People's Temple members would feel a sense of great indebtedness to Jim Jones, who had supposedly saved their lives. Jones would then document such instances of salvation, to be reciprocated later when Jones wanted Temple members to perform some favors for him.

Again, it is sometimes difficult to distinguish legitimate uses of influence tactics, such as the reciprocity rule, from illegitimate and exploitative uses. A good leader should use reciprocity in a fair manner. That is, the leader should not gain at the followers' expense. The leader should also provide for the actual needs of the groups, whether that be helping them to attain some desired goal, or representing their common interests.

Another powerful rule used in social influence is referred to by Cialdini as *the principle of commitment and consistency.* Generally, consistency is felt to be a good thing. We strive toward personal consistency in our behavior. It is important that our actions are, to a certain extent, predictable and fairly regular. People who behave inconsistently, changing their minds constantly, may be viewed as wishy-washy and indecisive. This striving toward personal consistency becomes an automatic response, involving every area of our lives. We automatically fall into consistent routines—always driving the same way to work, eating at the same restaurants, and espousing political opinions consistent with our general political attitudes and political party affiliations.

People place great value on consistency. I remember an instance where a governor of a state had come out in vehement opposition to an initiative that was on the ballot. The initiative was later voted in. A few friends and I were watching a news interview of the governor soon after the election. He was being asked what he intended to do about the initiative. The governor stated that he would do all in his power to see that the new initiative was swiftly and smoothly put into place. He would abide by the will of the people. Two of my friends started ridiculing the governor, calling him wishy-washy and accusing him of being two-faced. It was clear that they were upset by his inconsistent behavior, in spite of the fact that the governor appeared to be doing what his job called for, responding to the wishes of the majority of his voters. Often, people value politicians and leaders who are highly consistent, those who stick to their guns in spite of resistance. At the same time, we tend to believe that politicians who change their stance on an issue are weak. But ''blind'' consistency can be just as bad as arbitrarily changing one's mind.

In everyday life, people cling tenaciously to consistent patterns of behavior, for no other reason than ''this is the way I've always done it.'' Such blind consistency can interfere with an individual's ability to change and innovate. Quite often, we see people working in business or in their homes using very inefficient methods for getting a task done. They continue to use their old-fashioned strategy when a new one would work better.

I remember an old statistics professor who was still using a slide rule to make dozens of mathematical calculations. When we suggested that he use an available calculator, he replied, "This way is faster for me." He was not convinced until a graduate student challenged him to a contest. The professor was still working on the first few figures as the student's computer printer began to spew out reams of completed calculations. People sometimes cling stubbornly, almost superstitiously, to old, outdated habits, and tend to resist constructive change.

In order to use the consistency principle to influence others, the key is to get the person *committed* to a particular view or course of action. Once the individual has started moving in a particular direction, the consistency principle will take over, and future behaviors tend to follow in suit. Sometimes, the process of commitment and consistency is so strong that we find ourselves following a course of action that we had absolutely no desire to take.

A few years ago, I was having lunch in a coffee shop. From the other side of the restaurant, a woman started screaming, "Somebody help him. He's choking!" Instinctively, I jumped to my feet and started to move in the direction of the woman's screams. Then I started to think, "What am I doing?" I don't know anything about saving someone who's choking. I'd better sit back down and let someone else handle this." But it was too late. All eyes in the restaurant were riveted on me. No one else was moving. I could have sat back down, or pretended that I was simply making a sudden dash to the rest room, but I didn't. I had already committed myself to helping. With ambivalent feelings, I continued moving in the direction of the man who was on the floor. Trying to look like I knew what I was doing, I told a nearby waitress to call an ambulance. I rushed to the fallen man, trying to decide what to do next. Luckily, by the time I got to his side, the piece of food he was choking on had become dislodged and he was breathing again. Once committed, it is very difficult to break away from the pattern of consistency.

Salespersons often use the commitment and consistency principle to get you to buy a product. They begin their sales presentation by getting you to commit yourself to voicing an attitude consistent with purchasing the product.[8] A typical sequence usually goes something like this:

Salesperson: "Good afternoon sir. Are you concerned about the cleanliness of the drinking water in your area?"

Consumer: "Yes." (Isn't everybody?)

Salesperson: "Then you've heard about some of the many problems we've had in the area with water pollution, mineral deposits, and other sorts of contaminants in our drinking water?"

Consumer: "Yeah." (I think so.)

Salesperson: "Wouldn't you like to be able to do something to make your water cleaner and more healthful?"

Consumer: "Yes." (Of course.)

Salesperson: "Well, we'd like to allow you the opportunity to have cleaner water with our patented Aqua Pura water-filtration system, at no charge. We will install this device and let you use the system for two weeks with absolutely no cost to you. You do want to take advantage of this free, no-obligation offer to protect your health and that of your children, don't you?"

You get the idea. By tricking potential customers into committing to opinions concerning cleaning up the water, the salesperson is trying to trigger a pattern of consistent behavior that will eventually lead to an acceptance of two-week trial use of his product. At the end of the trial period, the customer is subjected to another sales pitch that will start by trying to get the customer to commit to the fact that the system works well. The consistent outcome is to purchase the product that you have already been using. Not only has the salesperson triggered the commitment and consistency principle, but by offering free use of the product, the reciprocity rule has also been called into play. The combined result is usually very effective.

Charismatic leaders often recognize the power of commitment and consistency and try to use it to influence followers. Devotion and loyalty to the cause are essential if the group is to achieve its goal. Loyalty oaths, initiation procedures, and program indoctrination are all techniques that are used by leaders to try to build commitment to a cause. But building a dedicated following is not an immediate process. It is done step by step, using the charismatic leader's persuasive communicative skills, along with tactics of social influence and manipulation.

Hitler did not suddenly order his subordinates to begin herding the Jews and other unfortunate groups into concentration camps and gas chambers. It was a process begun by simply getting followers to voice anti-Semitic feelings. Once Nazi party members had committed themselves, the next step was to have subordinates harass Jewish citizens and begin to strip them of certain legal rights and privileges. Once the pattern of oppression was begun, it was easier to get followers to engage in acts of physical violence and eventually to incarceration and murder. Hitler himself may have been caught up in a program of commitment to anti-Semitic actions that escalated and worsened as the years went by.

> The racial policy that the Nazis had conducted since 1933 had already led to frightful results: the Jews within the Reich had been systematically persecuted, frequently brutalized, sometimes murdered, and fully deprived of both their livelihoods and their civil rights. Now under the cover of a major war, Hitler was able to convert his wildest phantasies into a horrible reality . . . In the concentration camps and prisons of the Reich, before the firing squads of the SS execution teams, and in the great extermination camps of the east the Government of the Third Reich, under Hitler's authority, carried out the most enormous program of human slaughter of all time. This stupendous evil—the systematic murder of several million people, Jews as well as other racial or political "undesirables"—was the terrifyingly logical outcome of the irrational ideology that Hitler had developed during his formative years.[9]

When people think of the power that a charismatic leader has over followers, they are not greatly amazed that a strong charismatic leader can inspire a crowd to take positive action. After all, the leader and followers truly believe in the cause and in its moral goodness. People will fight for what they believe in. The mystifying part is understanding how a charismatic leader can get followers to perform some obviously evil action. The simple (and incorrect) explanation is that the followers of an evil charismatic leader must themselves be evil persons, but this is clearly not the case. Although Adolf Hitler and Jim Jones may have had many corrupt and wicked henchmen, many of the followers of these leaders were basically good, honest people. How is it then that normal, decent individuals will follow the orders of a malevolent leader when they may have serious doubts about the morality of their actions?

We have already seen that followers may engage in questionable behavior because they feel indebted to the leader or because the followers have already gotten themselves in over their heads through a process of commitment and consistency. And, of course, the leader can use coercive power—threatening physical harm to followers or to their loved ones unless they carry out orders. But these processes do not account for all the seemingly blind compliance to an evil leader's wishes. Two additional social rules help to explain why followers sometimes ignore the objections of their own consciences and, against their better judgments, carry out evil, destructive actions at a charismatic leader's bidding.

From our earliest youth, we are taught to respect authority. We follow the instructions of our parents and teachers, and we obey the order of traffic policemen, work supervisors, and government officials. *Obedience to authority* is a very strong social rule. The power of the obedience rule was illustrated in a series of studies by Professor Stanley Milgram of Yale University.[10]

In these studies, groups of men were recruited, through newpaper ads, to participate in an experiment studying the effects of punishment on learning. Arriving at the laboratory for the experiment, each participant was greeted by the experimenter—an ordinary man in a white lab coat—and by another research participant. This second man, a kind-looking middle-aged fellow, was actually an actor who would help set up the scene for the experiment. By a rigged drawing, the participant was assigned the role of Teacher, while the actor was to play the role of the Learner. The experimenter then led both Teacher and Learner to a room where the Learner was strapped to a chair, with an electrode placed on the Learner's arm. The Teacher was then placed in another room and seated before an ominous-looking panel of switches labeled SHOCK GENERATOR. The labels on the series of switches ranged from 15 to 450 volts, at 15-volt intervals, with accompanying descriptions of slight shock, moderate shock, strong shock, very strong shock, intense shock, extreme intensity shock, danger-severe shock. The 435-volt and 450-volt switches were simply labeled xxx!

The experimenter then explained that the Learner was to memorize a series of word pairs. The Teacher's task was then to test the Learner by asking him to remember the paired words. Any error would result in the Teacher administering a punishing electric shock to the Learner. On each successive error the punishment was to increase 15 volts. At this point in the instruction the Learner stated that he was concerned about the effects of the shock and mentioned he had a slight heart condition. The experimenter replied that although the shocks may be painful, they are not dangerous and should not cause any permanent damage. To increase the realism of the experiment, the Teacher was administered a sample shock of a mere, but painful, 45 volts.

The learning experiment soon begins. Unfortunately, and as planned, the Learner is not the best of pupils. He makes several mistakes and with each wrong answer, the Teacher administers a stronger shock. At 75 volts, the Learner can be heard moaning through the wall. At 120 volts, he complains about the painfulness of the shock. The 150-volt shock is a critical point in the experiment. Here the Learner demands to be let out of the experiment. The shocks are painful and the Learner says that his heart is beginning to bother him. Typically, the Teacher would turn to the experimenter.

"Please continue," is the experimenter's scripted response.

"But he doesn't want to go on."

"The experiment requires that you continue."

"You heard him complaining about his heart. We should stop," the Teacher pleads.

"It is absolutely essential that you continue," is the experimenter's matter-of-fact reply.

In most cases, the Teacher reluctantly continues to follow the experimenter's orders. At 270 volts, the Learner screams in pain. At 300 volts, he begins to bang on the wall. Each time the Teacher tries to stop, he is met with the experimenter's standard reply. "You have no other choice, you must go on."

At 330 volts, the Learner cries out in agony and refuses to answer any more questions. The experimenter instructs the Teacher to assume that silence is an incorrect reponse and to continue increasing the voltage of the punishments. How long does this go on? The sad truth is that nearly two-thirds of all participants in the experiment continued to obey the orders of the experimenter and delivered dangerous and painful shocks right up to the 450-volt level!

The majority of research subjects continued to inflict apparent harm on a helpless, innocent victim at the mere instructions of a presumed authority figure. (Of course, the experiment was completely staged. The Learner did not actually receive any electrical shocks.) If people carry out such deadly acts at the bidding of a nondescript, anonymous stranger, imagine the power that a charismatic legitimate authority figure might have over his followers. The murderous deeds performed by Hitler's soldiers and Jim Jones's henchmen are not as hard to believe (especially considering that they also had coercive power over their subordinates) when seen in light of the results of the Milgram experiments. A Hitler or a Jim Jones can use coercive tactics to get followers to obey orders, but in many cases they would not need to. Authority alone may be enough for a leader to influence followers. Imagine if a representative of the government contacted you and asked for your help in giving your time to ''help your President and your country.'' Or better yet, if the President himself called and asked for a favor. It would be hard to resist because of the tremendous authority the federal government and the office of the President carry.

A final tactic of social influence that serves to increase the power of charismatic leaders if called *social proof.* As much as people like to consider themselves independent and free thinkers, there is a great deal of evidence that we tend to follow one another. People are more similar in their actions than they are different. We often conform our behavior to the behavior of others, particularly when we are in an unfamiliar social situation.

I once overheard a conversation between two students who had both attended a Roman Catholic wedding service for the first time. One student remarked that he had been confused by all of the standing, sitting, and kneeling that the congregation did at different times throughout the ceremony. The second student replied that it had not been a problem. He had simply watched the people around him and imitated their actions. Many times, when in unfamiliar situations, we look to others for social proof and conform our behavior to what others seem to be doing.

The wise charismatic leader realizes the value of social proof and may use it to good advantage. Evangelist Billy Graham and other preachers call on the principle of social proof to get potential converts to come forward and identify themselves so that they can be brought into the fold. During the Billy Graham Crusade, counselors are "seeded" in strategic locations throughout the crowd and folllow a scripted sequence for moving forward toward the center of the auditorium or arena in response to Graham's request for people to "come forward to Christ." The effect is such that it gives the appearance of a massive, spontaneous response to his invitation. Members of the audience are presented with a scenario in which it appears that moving toward center stage is the appropriate and acceptable thing to do. Once they arrive on the arena floor, they are engaged by one of the counselors, who helps to initiate the new recruit into the following.

> Unless an outsider or observer of these events has been instructed to look for the name tags and ribbons worn by those moving forward (designating counselors), it is all too easy to infer from these appearances the "charismatic" impact of Graham and his invitation. These strategies promote the respectability of making a public commitment and represent methods calculated to manipulate the consent of the passive, the uncertain, the wary, and the indecisive.[11]

It is unlikely that many people in such large public meetings would come forward on their own, but the social proof provided by the counselors is a very effective and persuasive influence tool.

It has been reported that some pop performers and rock and roll bands have used similar methods to influence crowds to distinctive display of fan support. Supposedly, the management team of the Beatles hired women "screamers" and "fainters" for the group's early concerts and placed them throughout the crowd. It did not take long for the screaming and swooning to catch on, and soon the crowds began to behave in the expected fashion without the instigation of the paid supporters.

It is the principle of social proof that accounts for the phenomena at Jonestown and in the Nazi concentration camps where victims systematically went forward to their deaths without resistance like sheep to the slaughter. Some people have mistakenly assumed that these unfortunates were subjected to mass hypnosis. Others blame the victims, saying that they were weak and conforming persons without wills of their own. It is often asked, ''Why didn't they resist? Why didn't these persons, faced with inevitable death, rush en masse and overpower the few armed guards?'' A large part of the answer is that the social proof provided was not resistant behavior, but passive submission. The tendency to look to others for cues of behavior was in operation. As the first few victims moved forward, they set an example of the expected behavior for those behind to follow.

The tactics of social influence we have been discussing are but a few of the strategies used by leaders to gain control and influence over followers. The tactics themselves are neither good nor bad. They are basic principles of human social behavior. We all are subject to them. It is the uses that the rules are put to that are good and evil.

Because charismatic leaders are highly socially skilled, they are more apt to use these social influence tactics (and they are able to use them more effectively) than nonskilled persons. Unfortunately, as we have seen, some charismatic leaders use such influence techniques to evil ends.

How do we combat the evil use of influence tactics? The first step is to learn more about them. If we ourselves become skilled and knowledgeable in the use and abuse of such social rules we are likely to develop strategies that allow us to resist them.

The truly evil use of charismatic power is rare. More often than not, the use of charisma and social skill leads to positive, beneficial outcomes. Before we examine ways to increase charisma, let's talk about some of the ways that charisma can be used for good.

CHARISMA AND OVERCOMING SHYNESS

Perhaps the most obvious way that charisma can be used in a helpful, positive way is in the area of overcoming shyness, loneliness, and other social inhibitions. In his book, *Shyness,* Dr. Philip Zimbardo reports that 25 percent to 40 percent of all people consider themselves to be shy. A greater percentage state that they have at one time during their lives been shy.[12] Shyness as a social problem seems to be of epidemic proportions. (Zimbardo estimates that there may be as many as 84 million shy Americans!)

People who are shy have difficulty establishing and maintaining friendships and dating relationships. They report uncomfortable feelings of anxiety and embarrassment when in social situations. Shyness is often linked to depression, alcohol and drug abuse, sexual problems, and even suicide. On the more day-to-day level, shyness can inhibit one's ability to meet new people, to speak before groups (the number one fear of many people), and to feel self-confident.

To a great extent, shyness is caused by low levels of certain basic skills—the same skills that at high levels lead to the development of charisma. In fact, our research has shown that the higher a person's charisma potential, the less likely he or she is to be shy. Surprisingly, a great many of our famous charismatic people at one time (usually in their childhood or adolescence) considered themselves to be shy. Eleanor Roosevelt, Robert Kennedy, and Gandhi were all once shy individuals who forced themselves to overcome this handicap by developing their social skills. In these cases, overcoming shyness may have been a motivational force that led to the later development of their charisma.

It is important to mention that not all shyness is bad. As Zimbardo points out, the terms ''reserved,'' ''unassuming,'' and ''retiring'' refer to the positive aspects of shyness. Shyness, in part, stems from the basic skill of social sensitivity. Being socially conscious and concerned about the appropriateness of one's own social behavior is an asset if it is balanced by possession of expressivity and control. Social sensitivity becomes a problem when the basic skills are out of balance—the individual becomes overly self-conscious and socially anxious.

As psychologists are learning, one of the most effective ways to combat shyness is through social-skill training. The development of expressive skills both verbal and nonverbal, along with improving skill in emotional control and social acting, can overcome shyness. Taken further, developments of these basic skills leads to charisma. We'll talk more about social-skill training later.

CHARISMA, HEALTH, AND WELL-BEING

Earlier in this book, we discussed how charismatic physicians may have healthier patients as a result of patients' willingness to follow their medical instructions. But does charisma itself lead to better health? The answer appears to be yes.

Modern society has seen the emergence of a new, silent killer—stress. Stress has been called the "20th century disease."[13] It is quite well known that many types of life-threatening physical illness are brought on, or worsened, by stress. Heart disease, high blood pressure, ulcers, respiratory ailments, and diabetes are all stress related. Although we all may be exposed to stressors, such as work, family, and financial demands, not all persons succumb to these pressures and develop stress-related illnesses. Some people make themselves resistant by developing skills for coping with stress.

There are many ways that people try to cope with stress. they can take some kind of action to try to get rid of the source of the stress. They can turn to a friend or loved one to get some assistance in dealing with the problem, or simply to discuss the stressful situation. People may try to distort the situation—convincing themselves that the stress is not really a problem or even denying that it exists. Some people try to escape, others simply ignore the stress. Still others may try to get rid of the arousal caused by the stress through meditation, exercise, drugs, alcohol, or trying to relax. But what kind of coping technique works best? The success of a coping technique depends on the type of stress, the situation in which it is used, and the person's ability to use it.[14]

Our research indicates that socially skilled, charismatic persons may be better at coping with stress (and are thus healthier) than persons who lack basic social skills. One reason for this advantage is that if the stress arises from some interpersonal conflict—for example, problems with an irate spouse or a demanding work supervisor—the socially skilled person is well-equipped to take some actions toward successfully alleviating the problem, and therefore, the stress.[15]

Charismatic persons are also better able to call upon others for assistance in helping to overcome stress than are persons lacking in basic social skills. Years ago it was suggested that people who had large social-support networks (i.e, friends, neighbors, or relatives on whom they could call during difficult times) tended to experience less stress, and less stress-related health problems, than persons who did not have a great deal of social support. Some researchers found evidence for these "stress-buffering" effects of social support. However, the results of other studies failed to find such positive effects, and in a few studies people with close social support networks had *more* stress than those persons without much support.[16] Why the confusion?

It seems that what determines whether social support will be helpful or harmful in dealing with stress is whether individuals can adequately *use* their social-support systems. Other people can only help us with our problems when we have clearly communicated to them what the problem is, and when we have made it clear that we invite assistance in trying to cope with it. Persons with good communication skills will have an advantage here.

In some cases, social support, no matter how well intentioned, can only make the situation worse. For example, an overprotective mother who tries to help her shy child deal with stressful social situations by accompanying him to school parties and gatherings may only cause the child embarrassment and increase his stress level. The same is true of the friend who continually tells you, "I told you so,"—after the fact. In such situations, it is the socially skilled individual who will be able to say, "No thank you. I'll deal with this myself," without offending the well-intentioned would-be helper.

Another term for social skills is social competence. Socially skilled persons are competent at dealing with difficult situations, such as those that cause everyday stress. Charismatic persons are more than just socially competent. They excel in social situations. They have an ability to take situations that most people consider stressful and turn them into a challenge—an obstacle to hurdle, a puzzle to solve.

More than a dozen years ago, physicans Meyer Friedman and Ray Rosenman described what has been called the Type A behavior pattern, or Type A personality.[17] Type A people are hard-driving and competitive. They are ambitious persons who have a sense of time urgency—they are always racing to get things done. The stereotype of the Type A personality is a hard-working male (most of the research on Type As has been done on men) business executive. Type Bs are at the other extreme. They are easygoing and slower paced in their approach to life. To use a popular term, Type Bs are laid back.

The importance of the identification of Type A personality is that Friedman and Rosenman discovered a link between Type A behavior and coronary heart disease. For example, in a study of thousands of men followed for more than eight years, it was found that Type As had twice the risk of having a heart attack then did Type Bs.[18] On the surface, this looks like a bad situation for the hard-driving, workaholic Type A, but not necessarily.

Very recent research on the Type A personality indicates that only certain Type As have increased risk of heart disease.[19] In these studies, men were given tests to determine whether they were Type A or Type B. They also completed the ACT (Affective Communication Test), one of the brief measures of charisma that we discussed earlier. The Type A men were then divided into two groups, those who scored high on the ACT, and those receiving low ACT scores. As you recall, high ACT scorers are emotionally expressive, charismatic, and socially skilled. Low ACT scorers lack basic components of the social skills underlying charisma. All men in the study were then measured on a number of heart disease risk factors—such as blood pressure and serum cholesterol—all known to play a role in later heart attacks. The results showed that the low—ACT scoring Type As had a greater risk of heart disease than the high—ACT Type As. Although they possessed the coronary-prone, Type A behavior pattern, charismatic Type As seemed to be more resistant to potential coronary health problems than the noncharismatic Type As. In fact, the charismatic Type As were less coronary-prone than some of the Type Bs. Later studies have found similar patterns of results while looking at actual incidence of heart attacks, rather than just coronary risk.[20] Why would charismatic and noncharismatic Type As differ?

Some health researchers believe that Type A people are characterized by an effort to maintain control over all aspects of their lives. The Type A executive for example, tries to keep a watchful eye on everything that is going on in the office, controlling and coordinating the activities of all workers—a very demanding task to be sure! But if you remember something we said earlier, the key to a successful manager or executive is the ability to communicate. The executive is only going to be able to control the work environment to the extent that he or she is able to coordinate activities by giving clear and unambiguous orders, by soliciting important feedback from co-workers, by being persuasive and motivating, and by being sensitive to worker's needs. All of these tasks require good communication skills, and the charismatic executive is an expert in these areas. The charismatic Type A executive is able to get the job done (and research shows that Type As are generally successful— all that energy does indeed pay off!) but in a way that does not place tremendous strain on him and his heart.

On the other hand, the Type A executive who is a poor communicator gives orders that are unclear, and when subordinates mess up the job, the executive experiences a frustrating loss of control. The noncharismatic, nonexpressive Type A executive is unable to inject emotion into his or her dealings with workers, which often leads to workers' perception that the boss is insensitive and uncaring of their concerns and feelings. Lack of skill in emotional control can also lead to the executive flying off the handle, yelling at subordinates and making emotion-based and impulsive work decisions that may further alienate workers. The nonsocially skilled Type A executive strives to maintain control of the work environment and keep levels of production high, but the communication breakdown works against this. The executive feels frustrated and stressed. The wear and tear on the body (particularly the heart) begins, and over time, may lead to a system breakdown.

Although we are just beginning to do research on the links between charisma and physical and psychological health, the early results do indeed indicate that charisma can have some beneficial side effects in these areas.

Charisma, if used properly, is no doubt a good thing. Being more socially skilled and being a more effective communicator is a goal we all share.

So far, we have seen what charisma is. We have broken it down into its components and discussed each separately (this will come in handy later). We have also seen how it is used in politics, in business, in relationships, and for good and evil ends. The next section deals with how to get it and offers suggestions and techniques for increasing charisma.

✤ III ✤

Charisma:
How to Get It

❊ 9 ❊

Increasing
Charisma

A few years ago, signs started appearing around the University of California—Riverside campus:

Become *MORE CHARISMATIC* this quarter! A group of UCR researchers are searching for a limited number of volunteers for a study on the training of emotional expressiveness. The training will be fun and interesting for you, and just may increase your charisma. Hurry! Training begins soon!

We have been discussing charisma—defining it and seeing how it is used by charismatic leaders as a powerful means of influencing followers. Yet, we all possess some charisma potential. Charisma is composed of basic social skills. Thus, by improving and refining these basic social-skill components, anyone should be able to increase charisma.

In the Riverside charisma training project, Professor Howard Friedman and his research team were recruiting participants for a study of charisma training.[1] The idea behind this "charisma clinic" was to see if charisma could indeed be learned through the development of basic social skills. In this study, the emphasis was on increasing emotional expressiveness, although many elements of basic social skills were also taught to students in the training program.

For the next several weeks, participants attended training sessions in which they engaged in a variety of exercises designed specifically to increase nonverbal communication skills. They examined the facial expressions of emotion, their meaning, and how to enact them. They viewed slides and training films and were taught to be aware of the nonverbal cues they were emitting. Participants also played nonverbal training games and took part in role-playing exercises. Most importantly, each participant was given homework assignments—exercises to practice in between the training sessions. These assignments included practicing what they had learned in the sessions, as well as trying them out on friends. To insure that participants did indeed follow through with their homework assignments, "buddies" were assigned to call and check on the completion of homework. To establish a basis of comparison, a second group of student volunteers did not, at first, receive any training.

Each participant was videotaped before any training began, and a second videotaping was conducted at the end of the training program. The videotaping tasks involved the participant pretending to be a recruiter for career positions with a department store. Each participant was given a recruitment flyer from the store, asked to study it, and then each gave a persuasive presentation to an audience of college seniors who would be applying for the positions.

The before- and after-training videotapes for the students in the training condition were like night and day. Those who before training had appeared nervous, quiet, and awkward, were now, just a few short weeks later, making forceful, animated, and persuasive presentations. There was little improvement in the group that received no charisma training.

Not only did the participants improve their performances in front of the camera, but many of the participants reported increased confidence and improved communication lines with friends, which they attributed directly to the effects of the training program. Two of the participants reported that they had been hired as resident assistants for the university dormitories—competitive positions, obtained through a series of hiring interviews. Both participants felt that the training had helped them to get the job.

Although this is only one example of success, my experience, and the experience of many other people involved in communication-skill training programs, is that training people to be more effective communicators leads to a very dramatic positive change. Participants in social-skill or communication training programs show rapid progress over a short period of time. Much of this is due to what I call the snowballing effect—as you increase individuals' social skills and encourage them to put these improved skills into immediate practice with homework assignments, they receive immediate positive social reinforcement from their friends and family. In short, others begin to respond favorably to the improvement in the individual's communicative abilities. As the person's communication skills improve further, they receive more positive reactions from others. What you get is a self-perpetuating system of continued improvement—the snowballing effect.

CHARISMA AND SOCIAL-SKILL TRAINING

When we first defined charisma, it was mentioned that charisma was made up of extraordinarily high levels (and a balance) of basic communication, or social skills. Charisma is really nothing more or less than well developed social skills. Many professionals in a variety of fields have found out basically the same things that we have been talking about, namely: (1) many mental health and social problems are the result of people's inabilities to communicate with each other; (2) social skills can be learned; and (3) development of social skills can alleviate many interpersonal problems and help enhance mental and physical well-being.

But it is only fairly recently that social skills and social-skill training have become serious topics of interest for behavioral scientists.[2] In effect, mental-health professionals were rather late in finding out what people like Dale Carnegie knew all along—that social skills could be taught in much the same way that children are taught to read and write.[3] The methods are fairly straightforward, but they require systematizing and a lot of work and dedication. Three basic principals are important in social-skill training programs.

First, learning to be socially skilled, like learning to read, is best done in a step-by-step process—breaking the global skill down into its smaller components. You do not teach a child to read by starting with *War and Peace.* The child begins at the basic level, learning the components of language—letters, then words—before moving on to sentence structure and grammar. In the same way, an individual must begin by developing the basic social-skill components before he or she can become a charismatic speaker, politician, or manager. This is largely what our basic social-skill framework is all about. We start by pinpointing basic deficiencies and imbalances and then work on developing these basic components using a systematic process.

Second, all training programs emphasize the importance of practice. Learning to be charismatic is just like learning to become a virtuoso violinist. It takes practice, practice, practice. Most social-skill training programs emphasize learning new skills in the workshops or training sessions, trying them out with the trainers or on other clients in role-playing or in-class exercises, and then practicing the new skills out in the real world.

Third, care must be taken to see that the acquisition and development of social skills is constantly reinforced. But, as we have seen, reinforcement is not often a problem. As people improve their social skills, they become more effective communicators, and others begin to respond favorably to them. Relationships get better. With improved ability to get along in social interaction, self-confidence increases. As an individual becomes more

socially skilled, he or she receives more and more positive social reinforcement from others—the snowballing effect.

STARTING OUT

Before anyone can begin to increase charisma, there are several rules that need to be considered. To help you remember these important rules, think of the word DESIRE, which is the first rule:

Dedication

Energy

Systematic approach

Individual development

Review of progress

Energy

As psychologists, psychiatrists, and others in the helping professions have found, for a person to change successfully he or she must have the desire to change. To become more charismatic, you must truly want it.

It was reported that as a young man, John Kennedy was intrigued by the concept of charisma, particularly the charisma possessed by motion-picture stars. Kennedy and a friend, Charles Spaulding, traveled to Hollywood to meet the future President's film idols.

> The two men made the rounds of Hollywood night life, rubbing elbows with Cooper, Clark Gable, and other stars: "Charisma wasn't a catchword yet, but Jack was very interested in that binding magnetism these screen personalities had. What exactly was *it*? How did you go about acquiring it? . . . He couldn't let the subject go."

> Hollywood stars fascinated him . . . they embodied what he was and what he wanted to become; they had qualities he wanted to acquire.[4]

Perhaps Kennedy's strong interest in charisma and his desire to be charismatic helped him to attain it. Strong desire is the starting point for anyone who wants to develop charisma.

Dedication: Truly charismatic individuals are relatively few simply because it takes time to develop the required social skills. Dedication and constant work are crucial to develop charisma fully. Persons who have made a lifelong habit of self-discipline, and increasing self-knowledge, may have an advantage. Developing and nurturing charisma takes tremendous attention and devotion.

Energy: Any significant amount of self improvement will not take place overnight. People always seem to be searching for the quick fix—the easy solution to a problem. Unfortunately, positive change requires a great deal of time and energy. Success is almost always a function of the amount of energy and hard work put into the endeavor, and so it goes with charisma.

Systematic approach: This is what our breakdown of charisma into its social-skill components is all about. It is an attempt to separate out the basic social-skill dimensions in order to spot certain skill deficiencies and target them for attention. Our research has shown that the systematic approach works well. In fact, professional actors and actresses tend to have well developed social skills, gained in large part through acting courses and workshops or through supervised experience. Actors and actresses as a group tend to have very high levels of charisma potential due to their systematic training.

Individual development: The assessment and development of social skills should always be geared toward the strengths and weaknesses of each individual. We use the Social Skills Inventory and its subscales (along with other assessment techniques such as interviews, videotaped interactions, etc.) to develop a profile of an individual. We then get an idea of where each person's social-skill strengths and weaknesses lie.

Review the progress: The development of social skills and charisma is a step-by-step process. Therefore, it is important to stop occasionally and review the progress that has been made in a training program. Often, social-skill training programs use a goal-setting procedure in which specific behavioral goals are set for each time period. At the end of the period, a review of progress takes place to measure success and offer constructive suggestions to overcome difficulties. Constant evaluation of progress is crucial for the continual development of social skills and charisma potential.

Energy: Again! We cannot reemphasize enough the importance of hard work to achieving charisma. It's not easy, but it is attainable!

Let us assume that a person has the desire to become more charismatic, is dedicated to a program of social-skill training, and is willing to invest the energy needed to increase charisma. How do we begin?

In keeping with our systematic approach, we begin by diagnosing current strengths and weaknesses. One way to do this is through standardized tests such as the SSI. A short version of the SSI was included at the end of the first chapter of this book. To score this test, turn to page 193. The total score on the SSI is a general measure of your charisma potential. Very high scores on the short SSI, from 100 to 120, indicate a great deal of charisma potential. Scores of 80–99 indicate moderate charisma potential. The average range of scores is from about 45–79. Persons scoring lower than 45 usually need a lot of work in basic social-skill development in order to increase charisma.

While each of the basic social-skill components is represented by different items on the short SSI, this particular test is really too brief to assess each separate skill accurately. However, responses to specific groups of items can give an indication of strengths and weaknesses in a particular basic skill.

The items are arranged together in groups of five. The first five items measure emotional expressivity; items 6–10 assess emotional sensitivity; 11–15, emotional control; 16–20, social expressivity; 21–25, social sensitivity; and 26–30, social control.

To explore for potential weaknesses, look for items for which you indicated "not at all like me"—the zeros or ones. Read over each of these items. Why did you respond this way? Has this area created any problems for you? Make a special note of any category that contained more than three zeros or ones.

By pinpointing possible social-skill deficiencies, it is easier to provide a starting point for improving specific basic social skills.

A second way to explore for possible weaknesses is to use what is called a "behavioral checklist." Read through the following list of social behaviors and note any that are particular problems for you. In parentheses are the abbreviations of the basic social-skill components that relate to being able to perform the behavior successfully. (EE = emotional expressivity; ES = emotional sensitivity; EC = emotional control; SE = social expressivity; SS = social sensitivity; SC = social control.) Particular social skills that come up often in your problem check list are the skills that should be targeted for improvement.

CHECKLIST OF SOCIAL SKILL RELATED BEHAVIORS

Instructions: Simply note which of the following behaviors usually presents a particular problem for you.

- Meeting new people. (SE)
- Speaking in front of groups. (SE, SC)
- Dealing with an upset friend or spouse. (ES, EE, SE)
- Asking someone for a date. (SE, EC)
- Getting really close to people. (EE, ES)
- Getting along with disliked colleagues. (EC, SC)
- Voicing displeasure with service at a hotel or restaurant. (EC, SE)
- Asking others for help or assistance. (EE, SE)
- Initiating conversations with strangers. (SE)
- Conversing at parties with people of different backgrounds and interests. (SE, SC)
- Returning something to a store. (EC, SE)
- Going before a judge. (SE, EC, SC)
- Telling a joke. (SE, EE, EC)
- Lying (hopefully, little white lies). (EC, SE, SC)
- Proper social etiquette. (SS)
- Admitting a mistake. (EE, EC)

- Explaining to an employee what he or she did wrong in a constructive way. (EC, SE)
- Giving a compliment. (EE, SE)
- Not crying at inappropriate times. (EC)
- Sympathizing with a grieving friend. (ES, EE)
- Interviewing for a new job. (EC, SE, SC)
- Breaking off a relationship. (ES, EC, SE, SC)
- Giving a rousing speech. (EE, SE)
- Coping with a crisis. (EC, SC)
- Being a good listener. (SS)
- Covering up feelings. (EC)
- Uncovering the subtle feelings of others. (ES)
- Being flirtatious or seductive. (EE, SE)
- Conducting an interview. (SS, SC)
- Reacting to the criticism of others. (EC, SC)
- Speaking spontaneously. (SE, SC)
- Acting out a role, as in a play or a game of charades. (EE, SE, SC)
- Being a go-between in an argument. (ES, EC, SE, SS, SC)
- Being called on to speak in a class. (EC, SE)
- Explaining things to people. (SE)
- Being a good salesperson; being persuasive. (SE, SC)
- Apologizing. (EE)
- Hosting parties. (SE, SS, SC)
- Breaking off a date. (SS, SC)
- Being comfortable in mixed crowds. (SC)
- Appearing socially graceful in unpleasant situations. (SC)
- Being a good loser. (EC)
- Expressing anger or resentment. (EE)
- Taking charge in an emergency situation. (SE, SC)
- Being of service to others. (ES, SS)

- Defending an unpopular point of view. (SE, SC)
- Dealing with an emotionally distraught person. (ES, SE)
- Seeing the perspective of others. (SS)
- Keeping a conversation going. (SE, SS)
- Graceful goodbyes. (ES, SS, SC)
- Turning acquaintances into friends. (EE, ES)

Now go back over the social behaviors you noted. If you checked "Initiating conversations with strangers," indicating that this presents a particular problem for you, increasing skill in the area of social expressivity (SE) can help to perform this social behavior better. If you have difficulty "Seeing the perspective of others," you may need to enhance your skill in social sensitivity (SS). By studying the behaviors that present problems for you, it is possible to get some idea of potential basic social-skill weaknesses. Note which show up often. In a short while, we will present some exercises designed to help develop each of the basic social skills.

DEVELOPING A PERSONAL CHARISMA TRAINING PROGRAM

Formal social-skill training programs use a variety of ways to diagnose social-skill deficits. They also have numerous techniques and exercises for enhancing social skills. Our own programs rely heavily on the use of videotapes, role-playing sessions, and take-home exercises. Formal training programs offer structure, the guidance of professionals, and assistance and support from others in the progam. However, responsibility for the development of social skills and charisma lies, for the most part, in the individual. Therefore, it is possible to develop your own personal charisma training program—but, remember, DESIRE.

THE IMPORTANCE OF APPEARANCE

In Chapter 4, we discussed the role that physical attractiveness and appearance play in charisma. Whether we like it or not, appearance does play an important part in how we are perceived by others, how they treat us, and in our own feelings about ourselves. People make all kinds of unfounded judgments about others simply because of their appearance: "He dresses sloppily, so his work is probably sloppy, too." "She's not very attractive, I'll bet she has difficulty relating to people." "That person is overweight, which indicates selfishness and a lack of self-control." "Someone who dresses like that couldn't possibly be any fun!" As much as we wish that people were not so unfair, it is difficult to change others' beliefs. In some cases, the best way to get by is to play the game. If you can avoid it, do not allow the prejudices of others to put you at a disadvantage.

Fortunately, many aspects of appearance can be changed, if we so desire. The first step is to do a self-assessment. How would you describe the way you look? How do you think other people see you? Most importantly, what does your appearance say to them? What kind of image does your appearance create in others' minds?

Study some recent photographs of yourself. Try to be as objective and unbiased as possible and determine the positive and negative aspects of your appearance. What are your best and worst features? What things about your appearance are you dissatisfied with? Which would you like to change?

Ask a close friend or friends to do assessments of your appearance also. Have the friends think back to when they first met you. What was their impression of you at the time, and why? If they were you, would they change anything about your appearance?

Use a chart like the one below to assess your appearance.

Feature	How I Feel About It	Image It Creates	Would I Like To Change It?
Weight			
Figure/Shape			
Hairstyle			
Miscellaneous			

Weight. Are you happy with it? Would less or more weight make you more appealing, make you feel better about yourself, and give you more self-confidence? If you are committed to a program of gaining social skills and charisma, why not channel that commitment and dedication into two programs—social-skill development and controlling your diet. Of course, the key question here is: Do you want to change? People may have some general stereotypes (often inaccurate) about how weight and other physical characteristics are related to personality, temperament, or abilities. But these stereotypes usually have importance only in the initial stages of an interaction. Obviously, a single physical characteristic such as being overweight or underweight is not going to keep anyone from developing charisma. The most important factor is how *you* feel about your appearance and whether changing your appearance will be an advantage. You must be completely honest with yourself.

Figure/Shape. To a certain extent, being in good physical shape—trim, good muscle tone, and so forth—is related to health. People who exercise regularly are healthier and live longer, and they may experience a number of positive psychological side effects in the areas of self-confidence and mental well-being. Western culture is becoming more and more fitness conscious, and many people believe in the adage that a "strong body means a strong mind." Joining a health club or exercise program can be of assistance in controlling your figure.

Hairstyle. Since hair can be cut, grown out, dyed, streaked, shaped, curled, or straightened, there is almost an infinite variety of hairstyles. Because we usually converse with people face-to-face, hairstyle is one of the first characteristics that we notice about others. Hairstyles can communicate (or be interpreted as communicating) many things, but of course, this is dependent on the times and trends, on your age, geographical region, nationality, and a variety of other factors.

Try to determine what your hairstyle says about you. Is your hairstyle appropriate for the kind of work you do and the kinds of people you interact with daily? How different or similar is your hairstyle to those of co-workers and friends? Do you want to stand out, or do you want to blend in with the crowd? Being very trendy or avant-garde with your hair can get you immediate attention, but is it the kind of attention you want? The stereotypes you *do* want to avoid are those associated with dirty, unkempt hair.

Keep in mind that haircuts and hairstyles can be used to highlight attractive features and hide less attractive ones. A good professional hairstylist can help you here.

Dress. Dress is the most easily changed aspect of our appearance. Think about your usual style of dress. What do you like and dislike about what you wear? Is it what you want? Is your wardrobe varied enough to fit all of the different types of social gatherings that you usually attend? Like other aspects of our appearance, dress can be used to communicate subtle messages to others. What does your clothing communicate to others?

There is no doubt that certain types and sizes of people should not wear particular styles. Also, some colors of clothing may go better with your particular skin tone and hair color. Many department and clothing stores employ fashion consultants, or have very knowledgeable salespersons, who can help you design a wardrobe for success.

The dress-for-success idea is based, in part, on wearing flattering clothing that is appropriate to the occasion. But perhaps the most important thing about dress is that you feel comfortable with your clothing and overall appearance. I remember a friend telling me that when she went to an important meeting or interview she would wear what she called her ''power suit.'' As she described it, she knew that the suit looked good on her, and it seemed to convey a sense of competence and being in control. Probably the most important aspect of the suit was that it made her feel comfortable and confident—and then her social skills took over.

SOCIAL SKILL EXERCISES

The remainder of this chapter lists a number of exercises, each designed to help develop a particular area of social skill. By increasing your skills in these basic areas, you can help to increase your charisma potential.

EXERCISES TO DEVELOP EMOTIONAL EXPRESSIVITY

The following exercises are designed to improve emotional expressivity, which involves the spontaneous expression of feelings. It is a vital component that gives life to our messages to others. It is emotional expressivity that distinguishes charismatic orators from mere public speakers.

Training people to be more spontaneously expressive is not easy. Unexpressive persons are often the product of many years of being told to keep emotions in check or to bottle up their feelings. While there are situations in which control of emotions is important, free expression of feelings puts life and color into your messages. Most importantly, there are many important social rewards to be gained by being more expressive. Others will understand you better, and they will often respond with their own expressions of emotions. The sharing of feelings, and touching another person at the deep emotional level, are among the greatest of human experiences.

Loosening Up

Some unexpressive people are so out of touch with their true feelings—they have buried their emotions so deeply—that they cannot even recall the last time they had an open emotional release of any kind.

One way to help to release these pent-up emotions is to allow them some free expression. The next time that you feel a strong emotion, go off by yourself to a private place and let it out. But remember to pay attention to how the feeling is released. What did it sound like? How did it feel? What happened to your face (expression) and body as you let the emotion out?

Many psychologists use a similar exercise involving two people who stand or sit facing each other and begin to release their feelings loudly in a barrage of words and emotions. Besides giving practice in releasing emotions, the exercise is a good ice-breaker for helping people feel comfortable with each other. (After this, simple conversation is easy!)

Getting Some Facial Feedback

Much of our own social-skill training involves the use of videotaped feedback. People are videotaped while being interviewed, expressing emotions, meeting others, or in various other role-playing situations. If you have a videocasette recorder and camera at home, use it. If not, make due with a tape recorder.

Watching yourself on videotape allows you the opportunity to see yourself as others see you. Many times, people we have worked with are quite surprised at their own image and behavior on the television screen. In situations in which they thought they were comfortable, they appeared very nervous (and sometimes vice versa). When they thought they were being very emotionally expressive in a role-playing situation, they appeared lifeless and deadpan. Feedback about your own behavior is critical to understanding yourself and to overcoming social-skill weaknesses.

Emotions are most easily expressed through facial expressions, tone of voice, and, to a lesser extent, with body movements and positions. It is very important that you study your own facial and body expressiveness and listen closely to your voice when communicating strong emotional messages. Learn to attend to the sound of your voice when you are joyous, anxious, or surprised. Practice trying to put more feeling into what you hear.

It is also important to learn how to be more facially expressive. Use a mirror. Now try to get yourself worked into an emotional state. Remember the last time someone made you enraged, or the surprise you felt when you unexpectedly ran into a long lost friend. Express the feelings in the mirror. Study the facial movements. Try to be more expressive. The key to this exercise is to learn how to master your own behavior. You can do this by paying attention to how your voice sounds and to how your face feels when you are experiencing strong emotions. Practice learning to link up the scowling or joyous face in the mirror with the feedback that you are receiving from the sensory receptors located in the muscles of your face. Right now we are trying to make your face more expressive—increasing emotional lability, a term we discussed earlier. Later on, awareness of facial feedback will assist in learning the skill of emotional control, but for now, let the feelings flow.

Try Wearing a Smile

To see the effect that emotional displays can have on others, try smiling and greeting strangers you pass on the street or the people you encounter in stores or on elevators. Note their reactions. Positive facial expressions can be infectious. Too many people walk around with blank expressions on their faces. Find out the powerful and pleasant effects that the expression of positive emotions can have on others as you watch their faces light up with a return smile and greeting. Some people (usually a small minority) will ignore you, or may keep their blank, expressionless face. Don't worry about them; you're learning to be more emotionally expressive.

Some researchers have theorized that one of the ways we actually experience emotions is through facial feedback.[5] That is, by putting on a happy, sad, or angry face, we may actually cause ourselves to feel some of the emotion that corresponds to our facial expression. If this is true, putting on a smile can't hurt (a painful face will do that), it can only help make you feel more positive.

Keeping an Emotional Diary

Another technique for improving your emotional communication skills is to keep a record of your emotions and of others' reactions to your expression of emotions. For a few weeks, keep track of the times when you experience strong emotions and try to express these feelings to a spouse or close friend. Record both your underlying feeling and the other person's reaction. Did the other person respond at all? Was his reaction favorable?

The process of obtaining feedback is critical to the development of emotional communication skills, but people do not often respond in words to the subtle nonverbal cues we emit. They often react in kind, also responding nonverbally. Therefore, it is important to become more aware of our nonverbal behavior and of the nonverbal feedback we receive from others.

If you live with another person, try this exercise: Each day, before you walk in the door, think about the emotions that you are feeling. Are you happy because of some triumph at work? Are you worried because of some bit of bad news you heard before heading home? Are you angry? Make an effort to try to communicate that feeling nonverbally once you enter the house (but don't exaggerate; be subtle, yet emotionally communicative). Now, walk in the door and greet your partner/ roommate. After a moment of casual chatter, ask the other person, "What am I feeling?" See if he or she picked up on your true feelings. Use the feedback to improve your emotional "sending" ability. By reversing roles, you can help to develop your skill in emotional sensitivity, or emotional "receiving" ability. Recall that we mentioned earlier that skill in emotional expressivity and emotional sensitivity often go hand in hand.

EXERCISES TO DEVELOP EMOTIONAL SENSITIVITY

Emotional sensitivity involves skill in reading the emotional and nonverbal communications of others. Part of the skill of emotional sensitivity simply involves learning to rely less on interpreting the verbal channel and attending more to trying to understand nonverbal communication—in other words, listening less to *what* is said and listening (and watching) more for *how* things are said.

Becoming a People Watcher

Often, people lack skill in emotional sensitivity because they have a tendency to focus much of their attention during social interaction on themselves. They listen to what *they* are saying, are concerned with what *they* will do or say next, and strive to be the center of attention. Learning to be emotionally sensitive involves becoming a good watcher and listener.

If your self-assessment of basic social skills indicates a deficiency in the area of emotional sensitivity, try to nurture this skill by attending more to others in social situations. Learn the value of becoming a good listener. Learn to listen to the subtle cues of emotion in others' tone of voice and facial expressions. If someone is discussing a movie or play they saw recently, listen and watch for cues of liking or disliking. Validate your interpretations with a question such as, "It sounds as if you really liked (disliked) that play. Was it one of the best (worst) you've ever seen?"

Watch two people interacting from a distance. Try to determine, from visual cues alone, what is going on between them. Are they in a heated argument, exchanging pleasantries, gossiping, and so forth? Check out your interpretation, if you can, by getting close enough to hear a little of the conversation.

Developing skill in emotional sensitivity is one kind of exercise you can do sitting down. Just find a comfortable bench in a crowded park, shopping mall, at a party, or near an outdoor café, and watch, listen, and learn.

Single Channel Television

This exercise is also designed to heighten sensitivity. Tune in to an episode of a dramatic television series (daily soap operas work well). Now, turn off the sound. Try to figure out what is happening simply from the nonverbal cues of facial expressiveness, gestures, and body movement. Pay particular attention to any emotions displayed. (This exercise also helps to increase social sensitivity.) The following day, watch the same show, but this time only listen to the audio part of the program (you can sometimes accomplish this by turning the brightness control down all the way, or you can turn the television around or shut your eyes). Listen closely to the emotional clues in the actors' tones of voice and the rhythms and pacing of their speech. Also listen to voice quality and to the kinds of things they say. See if you can determine the actors' ages and the type of characters they are playing (e.g., dominant, fatherlike, temptress, innocent young thing, bad guy). Be sure to check your success-failure rates. You might try just watching a particular daily program one day, just listening the next day, and then watching and listening on the third day.

When I was a graduate student studying nonverbal communication, I would spend the greater part of my day watching research participants interacting on television. My job was to code various types of nonverbal cues. Sometimes I would focus on certain gestures, other times I looked at particular facial cues, and still other times I would listen for specific audio cues or speech errors. When friends would ask what I was studying in school, I would reply, ``Nonverbal communication. You know, body language.''

Often they would say things like, ``I'd better watch out. You can tell what I'm thinking,'' or, ``What does it mean when people sit like this?''

I would respond by clearing up some of their misconceptions about nonverbal communication. (``It's not really a *language* in the same way as a speaker's words.'') I would also deny having any special skill at decoding nonverbal messages. (``It's my *job*. I just research nonverbal communication, I'm no master of it.'') And I truly believed what I said. But as the research work went on, I did find myself becoming more skilled at receiving and decoding nonverbal cues.

I would go to a party or other social gathering and was able to pick up on some of the subtle cues that others missed. Through the practice I was getting in my research work, I was able to increase significantly my skill in sensitivity. (Of course, since that time, we have developed more systematic, and much better, techniques for enhancing sensitivity.).

Decoding Emotional Faces

Research has shown that some people are better at recognizing facial expressions of emotions than are others. Below are a series of twenty-five expressions. Study each expression, and then write the emotion it seems to depict. The answers are on the next page.

Try your hand at drawing such cartoonlike expressions for various emotions. This exercise is not only fun, it can help increase your sensitivity to real emotional expressions.

EXERCISES TO DEVELOP EMOTIONAL CONTROL

The skill of emotional control involves the ability to stifle the spontaneous display of feelings and the ability to pose specific emotional states. There are many times in social situations where display of feelings are inappropriate or unwise. For example, in an angry discussion it may be advantageous to put your feelings on hold and present your arguments in a calm, rational manner.

1 2 3 4 5

6 7 8 9 10

11 12 13 14 15

16 17 18 19 20

21 22 23 24 25

Answers to Decoding Emotional Faces

1. angry
2. angry, upset
3. sheepish/embarrassed
4. happy, contented
5. sad
6. puzzled/uncertain, worried
7. pleasantly surprised*
8. upset, disgusted
9. angry
10. neutral (absence of emotion)
11. sad
12. worried, puzzled
13. suprised
14. happy
15. angry
16. fearful
17. angry
18. sly/devious
19. bored/disinterested
20. upset
21. tired, relaxed, relieved
22. disgusted
23. sad/distressed
24. surprised
25. fearful

*The most commonly confused emotions are happiness-surprise, fear-surprise, and disgust-anger.

Emotional expressivity and emotional control are in some ways opposites. If we are referring to the spontaneous expression of feelings, emotional expressivity is the on-switch, and emotional control is the off-switch. When it comes to posing emotions—displaying an emotion that we do not really feel—emotional control is both the on- and off-switches. As in all of our basic social skills, the key is balance. A charismatic person possesses a balance of expressivity and control.

Becoming an Emotional Actor

Being a good emotional actor means having the ability to convey a particular emotion on cue. When the lights go up, you act. To become a convincing emotional actor you need feedback. Here is where a video recorder, tape recorder, or even a mirror can help.

Collect some emotional passages or dialogue from a favorite novel. Now practice expressing the emotions over and over to your camera/microphone/mirror while reciting the passage. Pay attention to the feedback. Is your emotional acting convincing? Pay particular attention to the emotional cues in your facial expressions and tone of voice. Try to avoid hamming it up. Sometimes the most successful portrayals of emotions involve subtle, yet clear, cues of emotion.

Perhaps the best strategy is to take an acting class at a local community college or join a community theater group. The experience of acting in front of others can greatly enhance the development of emotional control, as well as improving a number of other basic social skills.

The Emotional Flip-flop

Many years ago, in a film class, I saw a fascinating student film project. The film consisted entirely of a close-up of a woman's mouth as she told a story about her early life experiences. The amazing thing was that she was telling the story in four different languages, almost simultaneously! During the course of her speech, the actress would instantly and flawlessly shift from English to French to Spanish to German—all within the same paragraph of her story. She was demonstrating a type of verbal/linguistic control that very few people possess. We came up with an exercise, designed to develop emotional control, that uses the same principle.

Make up a deck of flash cards, each with a particular emotion printed in bold letters. (You might begin with the basic emotions of happiness, anger, sadness, disgust, surprise, and fear. We use eighteen cards with each of the six basic emotions printed on three cards. Later, you might choose more complex emotional expressions such as pride, sarcasm, sympathy, concern, interest, sincerity, insincerity.)

Shuffle the cards and place the deck face down beside you. Choose a particular story that you know well or use any emotionally neutral written material (newspaper article, textbook, and so forth). Begin reciting/reading. Turn over the first card and continue the story, but now say the words while portraying the emotion written on the card. A few moments later, without hesitation, turn over the next card and change emotions. Practice making the transitions as quickly as you can. Also be sure to make your emotional acting as real and natural as possible. This exercise works best if you can record your acting for later review. The assistance of a friend who holds your emotional cue cards, changing them at his own discretion, makes the exercise easier and more effective.

EXERCISES TO DEVELOP SOCIAL EXPRESSIVITY

Charismatic people are fluent speakers. Moreover, they are skilled at introducing themselves to others, initiating and carrying on conversations, and speaking spontaneously on a topic. The following exercises are designed to enhance the skill of social expressivity.

Making Small Talk

One of the best ways to practice becoming a good conversationalist is to force yourself to talk to strangers. The next time that you are standing in a line, riding a train or bus, or at some kind of gathering, strike up a conversation with someone next to you. The weather, current events, the common experience you are having, are all good topics for such casual conversations. If at first you feel a bit uneasy about talking with strangers, do a little preparation beforehand. Develop a repertoire of opening lines. Think beforehand of a topic or topics that might be good for the particular time and situation. Giving someone a compliment is an easy ice breaker, as is asking for directions or assistance.

Once you have started the interaction, try to keep the conversation going for a bit. One of the best ways to keep conversations going is to ask the other persons questions about themselves. Try to be a good listener and to keep the conversation interesting and socially rewarding for both participants. Finally, learning to end a conversation gracefully is as important as a good beginning.

Learning Impromptu Speech

An important part of the skill of social expressivity is thinking on your feet—being able to speak spontaneously on a variety of topics. To practice impromptu speaking, come up with a list of controversial social and political issues. Write each topic sentence on an index card stating succinctly the issue and position. For example, "Drug abuse courses should be made mandatory in all schools"; "The fifty-five mile per hour speed limit is restrictive and should be abolished"; "The government should provide child-care assistance for working parents." On separate cards write the opposing positions. Shuffle the deck. Turn the top card over, read the topic sentence, and immediately begin speaking in support of the topic for two or three minutes. Turn over the next card and repeat the procedure.

Again, it is important to get feedback in order to go back over your speeches and correct mistakes. Your video or audio tape recorder can make the feedback process easier. As you review your impromptu speeches, make sure that your arguments make sense and that they follow some logical sequence. If you have visual feedback, look for nonverbal cues that may be distracting a listener (e.g., nervous movements, scratching, inappropriate facial expressions). Try to make your speeches as smooth as possible, as well as making your presentation pleasing to the ear and eye.

Often, the key to speaking spontaneously and being socially expressive is simply developing the willingness to say something. People are often reluctant to speak in front of others due to shyness, fear of embarrassment, or lack of self-confidence. Of course, when you do speak, it is important to have something to say. In the same way that emotional expressivity and emotional control complement each other and must be in balance, social expressivity and social control also go hand in hand. Social expressivity deals with speaking fluency, while social control involves control over verbal communication. In other words, knowing when to start and stop talking. We will discuss ways to enhance social control later.

Distraction-Free Speech

Long pauses, stuttering, repeating oneself, and incomplete thoughts or sentences all distract from the smooth flow of speech.[6] Cutting down on such speech disturbances can help to facilitate verbal fluency and enhance social expressivity.

Learning the proper pronunciation of words and increasing your vocabulary are also helpful in improving skill in social expressivity. Remember to be systematic. Use a dictionary and put yourself on a word-a-day (or two to five words-a-day) program, so that each day you learn the meaning and use of a new word. Courses in public speaking can also greatly assist in the development of social expressivity.

EXERCISES TO DEVELOP SOCIAL SENSITIVITY

The basic skill of social sensitivity deals with ability to read the subtleties of social interaction and a general knowledge of social rules. Increasing social sensitivity involves becoming a more astute observer of social life and improving your knowledge of the rules that govern social behavior.

Becoming a Social Sleuth

Sir Arthur Conan Doyle's fictional detective, Sherlock Holmes, displayed extraordinary skills in social sensitivity. Through careful observation and clever deduction, Holmes is able to see things that others miss, and he routinely solves complex cases with only a seemingly limited set of clues.

The first step to increasing social sensitivity involves simply becoming more aware of what is going on around you—as Sherlock Holmes would say, ''improving your powers of observation.'' As we saw in regards to the skill of emotional sensitivity, you need to become a people watcher. However, rather than attending to the cues of emotion, social sensitivity deals with attention to the subtle cues that can disclose information about a person's background, social status, accomplishments, or intentions.

To become a better social detective, start to challenge yourself by setting up a set of social mini-mysteries to solve. The next time you are invited to a large gathering where you will be meeting some people for the first time, try to pick out who is who before you are introduced by using the information you already know about these persons. Cues of age, background, who each individual is interacting with, and the kinds of things that you overhear them say, may all prove to be informative cues to identity. Make a mental note of your choices, and keep score of your accuracies and your misses.

When you meet new people, use social cues to try to guess their occupations, whether they are married or unmarried, if they have any children, the region of the country they hail from, their interests or hobbies. The key to success is to make informative guesses, ones that you can justify on the basis of your observations, not merely going along with hunches or vague feelings about a person. Also, it is very important to review your progress continually, noting why you were correct and trying to discover reasons for inaccurate interpretations.

Asking Questions

In a novel social situation, a socially sensitive or charismatic person will feel a need to find out the particular social rules in operation in this new setting. Like an anthropologist discovering a new culture, the socially sensitive individual will ask questions of himself, and in puzzling conditions, of others, to find out what is going on in the unfamiliar environment. Once the new rules are known, it is easier to analyze and understand the behavior of others and to establish guidelines for one's own behavior.

When in doubt, learn to stop to examine a situation before taking action. Question the acts you are about to commit. A charismatic person's skill in the area of social sensitivity often keeps him or her from stumbling into awkward social situations. If you are truly bewildered in certain situations, consult books on social etiquette or consider taking an etiquette course.

The Movie Critic

To sharpen the skill of social sensitivity, learn to watch movies or television programs with a critic's eye. We have all seen films with very good or very bad acting, that are poorly written, with holes in the plots, poor dialogue, and inadequate character or story development. Learn to pay greater attention to what constitutes good and poor acting or good and poor script writing.

What are the cues that indicate that an actor is merely reading his lines? What are the inconsistencies in an actress's portrayal of a character? On the other hand, how can you tell when a great deal of effort (and money) went into a particular production? What are the elements that make some films classics? By learning to examine behavior in the way that a professional critic would, you will increase your ability to observe, your attention to detail, and your knowledge of appropriate and inappropriate social behaviors.

Using these same techniques, learn to analyze live performances from everyday life. What are the characteristics that make a good speaker? a good teacher? a responsive and caring physician? a knowledgeable and trustworthy financial adviser?

EXERCISES TO DEVELOP SOCIAL CONTROL

Social control is one of the most important of the basic social skills. Unfortunately, it is also one of the most difficut to develop. Social control deals with social role-playing skill—the ability to fit in comfortably in a variety of social situations. Social control also pertains to the regulation of speech, the ability to say the right thing at the right time, and skill in giving prepared presentations or speeches. Sociologist Erving Goffman says that much of our lives we play social roles.[7] When we come home from work, we switch from the role of professional in our field to the role of spouse, roommate, mother, or father. If our parents later drop by for a visit, we will switch immediately to the role of daughter or son. In other situations we play different roles. We are all fairly adept at playing these common, everyday roles. But how about the social role of host or hostess? Or the role of spokesperson for a professional group? Or the role of mediator in an argument? We may be less capable of dealing with these more specialized types of roles—here is where improving skill in social control can help.

Be Adventurous—Experience Life's Roles

Perhaps the surest way to become an expert social role-player is to get as much experience as possible in a wide variety of roles. Many of the famous charismatic persons mentioned throughout this book have had a tremendous range of positions and many opportunities to play different social roles. Theodore Roosevelt, for example, was a lawyer, cowboy, soldier, police commissioner, author, and naturalist, as well as President.

Try not to pass up any opportunities that might help to expand your role-playing skills. Nominate yourself for an office in a club or civic organization. Volunteer to make a presentation for your department at work. Organize and lead a group activity.

In the same vein, try to experience as many different types of people, cultures, and subcultures as you can. Learning how to fit in with different groups and different kinds of people is critical to the development of high levels of social control.

Learning to Think Ahead

Being tactful and socially diplomatic are also parts of the skill of social control. Many times people get themselves in socially awkward positions because they act impulsively—saying or doing the first thing that comes into their heads. Learn to get in the habit of pausing to reflect momentarily before you speak. Is what you are about to say sensible? Does it fit in with the course the conversation is taking? What will be the impact of your statement on listeners? Will your point be clear? Is now the time to say it? A brief pause to think before speaking can help avoid potentially embarrassing situations.

Similarly, the rule of thinking and preparing ahead also applies to formal talks and speeches. Being prepared and knowing thoroughly what you are going to talk about is critical to good public speaking. Adequate preparation also contributes to a feeling of confidence, and as people increase their skill in social control, they begin to feel more and more self-confident and in charge of social situations.

Social control, and all of the basic social and communication skills, can only truly develop through applying them in real-life situations. Exercises can help, but becoming more socially skilled and charismatic only happens through interacting with others. In a way, learning to become charismatic is like learning to play tennis. You can practice your stroke by hitting a tennis ball against a wall, you can jog to get in shape, and you can study books on proper tennis techniques, rules, and strategy. But it is only when you actually get out on the court and face a cunning and skilled opponent that you will begin to develop into a true tennis player.

Becoming charismatic means going out and getting involved in social life, putting your social skills to use to experience the excitement, the pleasures, the joys, even the pains and sorrows, of social life. Increasing charisma means increasing your ability to reach out and connect with others, and that is what being human is all about.

Appendix:
Determining your
Charisma
Potential

To score the short form of the Social Skills Inventory, simply add the numerical values of the thirty items together. The total score is an indicator of your charisma potential. As mentioned in Chapter 9, each five items on this test measure a specific social skill dimension. In other words, 1–5 deal with emotional expressivity; 6–7 measure emotional sensitivity; 11–15 assess emotional control; 16–20 deal with social expressivity; 21–25 measure social sensitivity; and 26–30 assess social control.

100–120 indicates very high charisma potential

80–99 indicates moderate charisma potential

45–79 indicates average charisma potential

Below 45 indicates that quite a bit of work is needed in basic social skill development to increase charisma.

Notes

For complete references, see Bibliography.

Chapter 1: Charisma: What Is It?

1. The earliest research on social intelligence is reported in Hunt (1928), E. L. Thorndike (1920), R. L. Thorndike (1936), Thorndike and Stein (1937). Guilford and colleagues also did work on assessing social intelligence in the 1960s; see Guilford (1967). O'Sullivan (1983), and Gibbs and Widaman (1982) give historical overviews of social-intelligence research.

2. There are a number of terms that are nearly synonymous with social intelligence—social competence, social skills, communication competence, etc. In his book, *How to Expand Your Social Intelligence Quotient* (1980), Dane Archer suggests, as we have, that social skills are components of social intelligence. However, Archer views social intelligence as being dominated by sensitivity skills. Our approach sees sensitivity as only about one-third of the skills that comprise global

social intelligence (the other components are expressivity and controlling skills).

3. The research on individual differences in communication skills referred to here involved work begun at the University of California—Riverside, under the direction of Howard S. Friedman. Some of this research is reported in Friedman, Prince, Riggio, and DiMatteo (1980), and in Riggio (1986). Also see Rosenthal (1979).

4. This short version of the SSI is included for illustrative and self-exploratory purposes only. It is not intended to be a substitute for the longer Social Skills Inventory. Additional information about the Social Skills Inventory can be obtained from: Consulting Psychologists Press, Inc., 577 College Avenue, P.O. Box 60070, Palo Alto, CA 94306.

Chapter 2: Charisma and Nonverbal Communication

1. It can be argued that it is nearly impossible to convey an emotion through purely verbal means. Unless the nonverbal cues are consistent with the verbal emotional label, the reported emotion may not seem credible. To find out more about nonverbal communication in general, see LaFrance and Mayo (1978). See Wolfgang (1984) for a bibliography of one hundred years of research in nonverbal communication.

2. Darwin's book was originally published in 1872 and was reissued in 1965.

3. Ekman (1973, 1980).

4. To find out more about the ACT, see Friedman, Prince, et al. (1980).

5. The transmission-of-emotion study is reported in Friedman and Riggio (1981). Maranon (1950) also discusses the process of emotional contagion.

6. The principle is the same for most any inspiring performance. Music fans will pay three to ten times the price of a record to see and hear their favorite musicians in a live performance. The visual emotions of the performers, the emo-

tional contagion of the crowd, and the sense of being at an event make it a much more emotionally satisfying (if only a one-time) experience.

7. See DiMatteo (1979); DiMatteo and Friedman (1982); Friedman, DiMatteo, and Taranta (1980); and Krupat (1986).

8. See Schlesinger (1965), p. 560.

9. Schlesinger (1965), pp. 673, 76.

10. For more information on the role of sensitivity in effective leadership and supervision, see Baron (1986), pp. 288–89.

11. Research with the PONS is provided in Rosenthal, Hall, DiMatteo, Rogers, and Archer (1979).

12. Description and use of the CARAT is in Buck (1976, 1978, 1984).

13. See King (1969).

14. For more information about the concept of self-monitoring, see Snyder (1974, 1979, 1987).

Chapter 3: Social Skills and Charisma

1. The topic of increasing social skills is considered in Chapter 9.

2. Mehta (1976).

3. A portion of the data on social expressivity and social networks is presented in Riggio (1986).

4. Many charismatic persons are distinguished by their knowledge and adherence to social rules. Charismatic persons are often described as cultured or refined. Learning the rules of appropriate social behavior for a given situation, or in a certain group or subculture, is a key element of charisma. Charm schools and courses in etiquette can help lead to the development of social sensitivity. The enormous number and type of social rules is reflected in the size and detail of many etiquette books. Moreover, there are etiquette books for just about every type of person imaginable. For example, there are etiquette books for men, for women, for children, for the

upper class, for social climbers—even etiquette guides for specific religious and occupational groups.

5. Research with the SIT is presented in Archer and Akert (1977), and in Archer (1980).

6. Lash (1984).

7. Youngs (1985).

8. It is interesting to note that a positive relationship exists between charisma (i.e., social skills) and *social* self-esteem. However, it is important to make a distinction between social self-esteem and internal, subjective feelings of esteem or self-worth. The socially skilled person may, at times, report feeling low levels of self-worth. However, the person remains confident in his or her abilities to succeed in social interaction.

9. This research was conducted by the author and Barbara Throckmorton. The results reported here are from Ms. Throck-morton's master's thesis (California State University-Fullerton, 1985). See also Riggio and Throckmorton (1987).

10. We have found that the expressiveness associated with charisma is conveyed through multiple channels—facial expressions, body movement, tone of voice. Eliminating certain cues—for example, tone of voice—lessens the person's charismatic influence. Some of this research was reported in Riggio (1986); Riggio and Friedman (1981); Riggio, Friedman, and DiMatteo (1981).

11. For a recent overview of research on ability to deceive, see DePaulo, Stone, and Lassiter (1985).

12. Ekman (1985), p. 263.

13. The results of these studies are reported in Riggio and Friedman (1983); Riggio, Tucker, and Throckmorton (1987); and Riggio, Tucker and Widaman (forthcoming).

14. For research on sex differences in nonverbal communication, see Mayo and Henley (1981), and Hall (1984).

15. See Riggio (1986).

16. This may relate to the fact that some charisma "power" may diminish as you get closer to the person. Two processes

may occur. First, you may habituate to the expressive style and communication skills of the charismatic person. Second, if you are close to the person, you see his human flaws clearly.

Chapter 4: Charisma and Physical Attractiveness

1. See Berscheid and Walster (1974, 1978). Also see Patzer (1985), and Reis, Nezlek, and Wheeler (1980).
2. See Dion, Berscheid, and Walster (1972). Of course, there can be a *reverse* halo effect, where a single characteristic can lead to an overall negative evaluation.
3. Berscheid and Walster (1978).
4. The dating study was conducted by Walster, Aronson, Abrahams, and Rottman (1966).
5. Mitchell (1936), pp. 122–23.
6. This clever experiment was conducted by University of Minnesota researchers Snyder, Tanke, and Berscheid (1977).
7. These studies were reported in Riggio (1986); Riggio and Friedman (1981 and 1986); and in a forthcoming report by Riggio and Tucker.
8. See Levinger and Snoek (1972).
9. Hatfield and Walster (1978).
10. The study of long-term marriages was reported in Traupmann and Hatfield (1981).

Chapter 5: Charisma, Leadership, and Political Power

1. Weber (1968), p. 241. By far, most research on charisma follows Weber's thinking. See for example Boss (1976), and Camic (1980). Another approach to the study of charisma derives from the Freudian school. See for example Schiffer (1973). However, the orientation of this book is quite different, concentrating on charisma as residing in the individual—an approach that crosscuts the fields of personality and social psychology.

2. White (1961), pp. 329–330.

3. C. S. King (1969), p. 239.

4. Schlesinger (1965), pp. 115, 285.

5. Schlesinger (1978), p. 600.

6. The two quotes from FDR were taken from Miller (1983), pp. 480, 481.

7. Kytle (1969), p. 142.

8. The eyewitness account of the Salt Marches comes from UPI correspondent Webb Miller, cited in Kytle (1969), pp. 142–43.

9. See Schweitzer (1974), p. 156.

10. Graves (1928), p. 234. Also see A. W. Lawrence (1937).

11. William T. O'Neil to J. S. Van Duzen, cited in Grantham (1971), p. 95.

12. Accounts of the 1960 presidential debates are given in Schlesinger (1965); Sorenson (1965); and White (1961).

13. Cannon (1974), pp. 50–51.

14. Ibid., p. 42.

15. Ibid., pp. 56–57.

Chapter 6: Leadership in the Workplace: The Charismatic Manager

1. See Mintzberg (1973).

2. See Baron (1986).

3. Ibid.

4. Abodaher (1982), pp. 8–9, 142.

5. Abodaher (1982), p. 142. See also Iacocca and Novak (1984).

6. Baron (1986), pp. 288–89.

7. The work on power bases comes from French and Raven (1959).

8. Some of this work was presented in a paper entitled "Communication skills in various occupational groups," presented

at the meeting of the Western Psychological Association, May 1986, in Seattle, WA. Additional findings were that, as a group, members of certain professions tended to have social-skill patterns appropriate to the type of work in which they were engaged. For example, counselors and persons in human-service professions tended to be high in sensitivity skills; salespersons were expressive. Managers, however, tended to possess high levels of skill overall and more balance among skills.

Chapter 7: Charisma and the Media

1. White (1982), p. 167.

2. Ibid., pp. 190–91.

3. Ibid., pp. 31–32.

4. See Riggio (1986).

5. Although these results have been widely reported, I have been unable to find any reports of controlled studies of the effects of the Kennedy-Nixon debates. The radio-television difference is probably based on anecdotal evidence.

6. Other researchers of emotional communication have discovered these "micro-expressions" (Ekman, 1985; Haggard and Isaacs, 1966), but they have not looked at individual differences in the display of these fleeting facial changes.

7. Reagan seems to have a unique sort of charisma. His particular blend of emotional expressiveness leads to perceptions of great trustworthiness. Even when he makes mistakes or slips of the tongue, Reagan remains surprisingly popular and well liked.

8. See Friedman, Prince, Riggio, and DiMatteo (1980); and Riggio (1986).

9. It is interesting that Carol Burnett and Alan Alda appear in our recent lists of charismatic personalities, as neither currently has a television show. However, their earlier shows still appear on syndicated reruns in many areas.

10. The term "mediated ministry" is borrowed from a recent issue of the *Journal of Communication* (1985, Vol. 35), which contained several articles on TV evangelists.

11. Horsfield (1984), pp. 7–8.

12. Horsfield (1984), p. 26. Also see Armstrong (1979).

13. See Hadden and Swann (1981). In an interesting article, Goethals sees a parallel between a preacher's interaction with a congregation and a press conference held by President Reagan.

14. Another recent issue of the *Journal of Communication* (1986, Vol. 36, No. 1) contains several articles with research on music videos.

Chapter 8: Charisma for Good and for Evil

1. *U.S. Naval Institute Proceedings*, (December 1953), cited in Stein (1968), p. 106.

2. C. S. King (1969), p. 273.

3. Eade (1953), pp. 77–78.

4. Dietrich (1957), p. 16.

5. Cialdini (1984).

6. Langer (1972), p. 45.

7. Mills (1979), pp. 122–23.

8. See Cialdini (1984).

9. Stein (1968), pp. 14–15.

10. The shock experiments are described in detail in Milgram (1975).

11. Altheide and Johnson (1977), p. 332.

12. See Zimbardo (1977). Also see Jones, Cheek, and Briggs (1986).

13. See Toffler (1970), and Albrecht (1979).

14. For more information about stress and coping processes, see Lazarus and Folkman, (1984).

15. Researcher Kenneth Heller first suggested that social skills might moderate the relationship between social support and

stress. See Heller (1979), and Heller and Swindle (1983). Our own work on the subject will be reported in forthcoming articles.

16. For a review of research on the interrelationships of social support, stress, and coping, see Shumaker and Brownell (1984–1985).

17. See Friedman and Rosenman (1974).

18. The longitudinal study of coronary-prone patients was reported in Rosenman et al. (1975).

19. See Friedman, Hall, and Harris (1985), and Friedman, Harris, and Hall (1984).

20. These results are reported in Friedman and Booth-Kewley (1987).

Chapter 9: Increasing Charisma

1. The UC—Riverside charisma training experiment is reported in an unpublished manuscript by Friedman, Nelson, and Harris (1984).

2. Recently, there has been an explosion in interest and research on social skills training from a number of disciplines. See Curran and Monti (1982); Trower, Bryant, and Argyle (1978); and Wine and Smye (1981). Although studied by different fields, the groups seem to be moving along parallel lines. Communication theorists speak of "communicative competence" and overcoming social skill deficits such as "communication apprehension." See Diez (1984); and Mc-Croskey (1977). Social psychologists use the term "social competence" and are concerned with helping people overcome "shyness" (Jones, Cheek, and Briggs, 1986; Zimbardo, 1977), "self-consciousness" (Buss, 1980), "social anxiety" (Leary, 1983), or "loneliness" (Peplau and Perlman, 1982; Rubenstein and Shaver, 1982). Still other researchers focus on the acquisition of "relationship skills" and the use of social skills to improve marriages, friendships, and work relationships (see, for example, Bornstein and Bornstein, 1986; Noller, 1984).

3. Carnegie (1936, 1956).

4. Collier and Horowitz (1984), pp. 148, 235.

5. The so-called "facial-feedback hypothesis" has been suggested by a number of researchers, although there is some disagreement about how important facial feedback is to the experience of emotion. See Buck (1984); and Ekman, Friesen, and Ellsworth (1972).

6. Although we have been taught that filling a pause with an "uh" or "ah" detracts from the flow of speech, some of our research indicates that this particular type of speech error may not be evaluated as negatively as other speech disturbances. The "uh" may act as a form of phrasing or punctuation. Also, a pause filled with an "uh" may be better than an empty pause, at least in terms of keeping the sounds of speech flowing. See Riggio and Friedman (1983, 1986).

7. See Goffman (1959).

Bibliography

Abodaher, D. *Iacocca.* New York: MacMillan, 1982.

Albrecht, K. *Stress.* Englewood Cliffs, NJ: Prentice-Hall, 1979.

Altheide, D.L. and **M.L. Johnson,** "Counting Souls: A Study of Counseling at Evangelical Crusades." *Pacific Sociological Review, 20,* 1977, pp. 323–48.

Archer, D. *How to Expand Your Social Intelligence Quotient.* New York: M. Evans, 1980.

——— and **R.M. Akert.** "Words and Everything Else: Verbal and Nonverbal Cues in Social Interpretation." *Journal of Personality and Social Psychology, 35,* 1977, pp. 443–49.

Armstrong, B. *The Electric Church.* Nashville, TN: Thomas Nelson, 1979.

Baron, R.A. *Behavior in organizations.* (2nd ed.). Boston: Allyn & Bacon, 1986.

Berscheid, E. and **E.H. Walster.** "Physical attractiveness." *Advances in Experimental Social Psychology, 7,* 1974, pp. 158–215.

——— and **E.H. Walster.** *Interpersonal attraction.* (2nd ed.). Reading, MA: Addison-Wesley, 1978.

Bornstein, P.H. and **M.T. Bornstein.** *Marital Therapy: A Behavioral-Communications Approach.* New York: Pergamon Press, 1986.

Boss, G.P. "Essential Attributes of the Concept of Charisma." *The Southern Speech Communication Journal, 41,* 1976, pp. 300–13.

Buck, R. "A Test of Nonverbal Receiving Ability: Preliminary Studies." *Human Communication Research, 2,* 1976, pp. 162–71.

———— "The Slide Viewing Technique for Measuring Nonverbal Sending Accuracy: A Guide for Replication." *JSAS Catalog of Selected Documents in Psychology, 8,* 1978, p. 63.

———— *The Communication of Emotions.* New York: Guilford Press, 1984.

Buss, A.H. *Self-consciousness and Social Anxiety.* San Francisco: W.H. Freeman, 1980.

Camic, C. "Charisma: Its Varieties, Preconditions, and Consequences." *Sociological Inquiry, 50* 5–23, 1980.

Cannon, L. "The Forces That Forged the Future." In *The Fall of a President.* New York: Delacorte Press, 1974.

Carnegie, D. *How to Win Friends and Influence People.* New York: Simon & Schuster, 1936.

———— *How to Develop Self-confidence and Influence People by Public Speaking.* New York: Pocket Books, 1956.

Cialdini, R.B. *Influence: How and Why People Agree to Things.* New York: William Morrow, 1984.

Collier, P. and **D. Horowitz.** *The Kennedys.* New York: Summit Books, 1984.

Curran, J.P. and **P.M. Monti** (Eds.). *Social Skills Training.* New York: Guilford Press, 1982.

Darwin, C. *The Expression of Emotions in Man and Animals.* Chicago: University of Chicago Press, 1965.

DePaulo, B.M., J.I. Stone and **G.D. Lassiter** "Deceiving and Detecting Deceit." In B.R. Schlenker (Ed.), *The Self and Social Life.* New York: McGraw-Hill, 1985.

Dietrich, O. *The Hitler I Knew.* London: Methuen, 1957.

Diez, M.E. "Communication Competence: An Interactive Approach." In R.N. Bostrom (Ed.), *Communication Yearbook 8.* Beverly Hills, CA: Sage Press, 1984.

DiMatteo, M.R. "A Social Psychological Analysis of Physician-Patient Rapport: Toward a Science of the Art of Medicine." *Journal of Social Issues, 35,* 1979, pp. 12–33.

DiMatteo, M.R. and **H.S. Friedman** *Social Psychology and Medicine.* Cambridge, MA: Oelgeschlager, Gunn, & Hain, 1982.

Dion, K., E. Berscheid and **E. Walster** "What is Beautiful is Good." *Journal of Personality and Social Psychology, 24,* 1972, pp. 285–90.

Eade, C. (Ed.). *Churchill by His Contemporaries.* London: Hutchinson & Co., 1953.

Eisler, R.M. and **Fredriksen** *Perfecting Social Skills.* New York: Plenum, 1980.

Ekman, P. (Ed.) *Darwin and Facial Expression.* New York: Academic Press, 1973.

——— *The Face of Man: Expression of Universal Emotions in a New Guinea Village.* New York: STPM Press, 1980.

——— *Telling Lies.* New York: Norton, 1985.

——— **W.V. Friesen** and **P. Ellsworth** *Emotion in the Human Face.* New York: Pergamon Press, 1972.

Fleming, G. *Hitler and the Final Solution.* Berkeley, CA: University of California Press, 1984.

French, J.R.P. and **B. Raven** "The Bases of Social Power." In D. Cartwright (Ed.), *Studies in Social Power.* Ann Arbor, MI: University of Michigan Press, 1959.

Friedman, H.S. "The Concept of Skill in Nonverbal Communication: Implications for Understanding Social Interaction." In R. Rosenthal (Ed.), *Skill in Nonverbal Communication.* Cambridge, MA: Oelgeschlager, Gunn, & Hain, 1979.

——— and **S. Booth-Kewley.** "Personality and Coronary Heart Disease: The Role of Emotional Expression." Unpublished manuscript, 1987.

———— **M.R. DiMatteo** and **A. Taranta** "A Study of the Relationship Between Individual Differences in Nonverbal Expressiveness and Factors of Personality and Social Interaction." *Journal of Research in Personality, 14*, 1980, pp. 351–64.

———— **J.A. Hall** and **M.J. Harris** "Type A Behavior, Nonverbal Expressive Style, and Health." *Journal of Personality and Social Psychology, 48*, 1985, pp. 1299–1315.

———— **M.J. Harris** and **J.A. Hall** "Nonverbal Expression of Emotion: Healthy Charisma or Coronary-Prone Behavior?" In C. Van Dyke, L. Temoshok, and L.S. Zegans (Eds.), *Emotions in Health and Illness: Applications to Clinical Practice.* San Diego, CA: Grune & Stratton, 1984.

———— **B.C. Nelson** and **M.J. Harris** "The Training of Personal Charisma." Unpublished manuscript.

———— **L.M. Prince, R.E. Riggio** and **M.R. DiMatteo** "Understanding and Assessing Nonverbal Expressiveness: The Affective Communication Test." *Journal of Personality and Social Psychology, 39*, 1980, pp. 333–51.

———— and **R.E. Riggio** "Effects of Individual Differences in Nonverbal Expressiveness on Transmission of Emotion." *Journal of Nonverbal Behavior, 6*, 1981, 96–102.

Friedman, M. and **R.H. Rosenman** *Type A Behavior and Your Heart.* New York: Alfred A. Knopf, 1974.

Gibbs, J.C. and **K.F. Widaman** *Social Intelligence.* Englewood Cliffs, NJ: Prentice-Hall, 1982.

Gifford, R., F. Ny and **M. Wilkinson** "Nonverbal Cues in the Employment Interview: Links Between Applicant Qualities and Interviewer Judgments." *Journal of Applied Psychology, 70*, 1985, pp. 729–36.

Goethals, G. "Religious Communication and Popular Piety." *Journal of Communication, 35*, 1985, pp. 149–56.

Goffman, E. *The Presentation of Self in Everyday Life.* Garden City, NY: Doubleday Anchor, 1959.

Grantham, D.W. (Ed.) *Theodore Roosevelt.* Englewood Cliffs, NJ: Prentice-Hall, 1971.

Graves, R. *Lawrence and the Arabian Adventure.* Garden City, NY: Doubleday, Doran, & Co., 1928.

Guilford, J.P. *The Nature of Human Intelligence.* New York: McGraw-Hill, 1967.

Hadden, J.K. and **C.E. Swann** *Prime Time Preachers: The Rising Power of Televangelism.* Reading, MA: Addison-Wesley, 1981.

Haggard, E.A. and **K.S. Isaacs** "Micro-Momentary Facial Expressions." In L.A. Gottschalk, & A.H. Auerbach (Eds.), *Methods of research in psychotherapy.* New York: Appleton Century Crofts, 1966.

Hall, J.A. *Nonverbal Sex Differences: Communication Accuracy and Expressive Style.* Baltimore, MD: Johns Hopkins University Press, 1984.

Hatfield, E. and **G.W. Walster** *A New Look at Love.* Reading, MA: Addison-Wesley, 1978.

Heller, K. "The Effects of Social Support: Prevention and Treatment Implications." In A.P. Goldstein & F.H. Kanfer (Eds.). *Maximizing Treatment Gains: Transfer Enhancement in Psychotherapy.* New York: Academic Press, 1979.

———— and **R. Swindle** "Social Networks, Perceived Social Support, and Coping with Stress." In R.D. Felner et al. (Eds.), *Preventive Psychology, Research, and Practice in Community Intervention.* New York: Pergamon Press, 1983.

Horsfield, P.G. *Religious Television: The American Experience.* New York: Congman, 1986.

Hunt, T. "The Measurement of Social Intelligence." *Journal of Applied Psychology, 12,* 1928, pp. 317–34.

Iacocca, L. and **W. Novak** *Iacocca: An Autobiography.* New York: Bantam Books, 1984.

Jones, W.H., J.M. Cheek, and **S.R. Briggs** (Eds.) *Shyness: Perspectives on Research and Treatment.* New York: Plenum, 1986.

Jourard, S.M. *The Transparent Self.* New York: von Nostrand Reinhold, 1971.

Keller, M. (Ed.) *Theodore Roosevelt: A Profile.* New York: Hill and Wang, 1967.

King, C.S. *My Life with Martin Luther King, Jr.* New York: Holt, Rinehart, & Winston, 1969.

Krupat, E. "A Delicate Imbalance." *Psychology Today, 20,* 1986, pp. 22–26.

Kytle, C. *Gandhi: Soldier of Nonviolence.* New York: Grosset & Dunlap, 1969.

LaFrance, M. and **C. Mayo** *Moving Bodies: Nonverbal Communication in Social Relationships.* Monterey, CA: Brooks/Cole, 1978.

Langer, W.C. *The Mind of Adolf Hitler: The Secret Wartime Report.* New York: Basic Books, 1972.

Lash, J.P. *Life Was Meant to be Lived: A Century Portrait of Eleanor Roosevelt.* New York: Norton, 1984.

Lawrence, A.W. (Ed.) *T.E. Lawrence: By His Friends.* London: Jonathan Cope Ltd., 1937.

Lazarus, R.S. and **S. Folkman** *Stress, Appraisal, and Coping.* New York: Springer, 1984.

Leary, M. *Understanding Social Anxiety.* Beverly Hills, CA: Sage Press, 1983.

Levinger, G. "Toward the Analysis of Close Relationships" *Journal of Experimental Social Psychology, 16,* 1980, pp. 510–44.

—— and **J.D. Snoek** *Attraction in Relationships: A New Look at Interpersonal Attraction.* Morristown, NJ: General Learning Press, 1972.

Maranon, G. "The Psychology of Gesture." *Journal of Nervous and Mental Disease, 112,* 1950, pp. 469–97.

Mayo, C. and **N.M. Henley** (Eds.) *Gender and Nonverbal Behavior.* New York: Springer-Verlag, 1981.

Mehta, V. *Mahatma Gandhi and His Apostles.* New York: Penguin Books, 1977.

Milgram, S. *Obedience to Authority.* New York: Harper Colophon, 1975.

Miller, N. *F.D.R.: An Intimate History.* Garden City, NY: Doubleday & Co., 1983.

Mills, J. *Six Years With God: Life Inside Rev. Jim Jones's Peoples Temple.* New York: A & W Publishers, 1979.

Mintzberg, H. *The Nature of Managerial Work.* New York: Harper & Row, 1973.

Mitchell, M. *Gone With the Wind.* New York: MacMillan, 1936.

Noller, P. *Nonverbal Communication and Marital Interaction.* New York: Pergamon Press, 1984.

O'Sullivan, M. "Measuring Individual Differences." In J.M. Wiemann and R.P. Harrison (Eds.), *Nonverbal Interaction.* Beverly Hills, CA: Sage, 1983.

Patterson, T.E. *The Mass Media Election: How Americans Choose Their President.* New York: Praeger, 1980.

Patzer, G. *The Physical Attractiveness Phenomenon.* New York: Plenum, 1985.

Peplau, A.L. and **D. Perlman** (Eds.). *Loneliness: A Sourcebook of Current Theory, Research, and Therapy.* New York: Wiley-Interscience, 1982.

Reis, H.T., J. Nezlek, and **L. Wheeler** "Physical Attractiveness in Social Interaction." *Journal of Personality and Social Psychology, 38,* 1980, pp. 604–17.

Riggio, R.E. "Assessment of Basic Social Skills." *Journal of Personality and Social Psychology, 51,* 1986, pp. 649–60.

——— et al. "Beauty is More Than Skin Deep: Components of Attractiveness." Paper presented at meeting of the American Psychological Association, New York, 1987.

——— and **H.S. Friedman** "Charisma and Initial Attraction." Paper presented at meeting of the American Psychological Association, Los Angeles, CA, 1981.

——— and **H.S. Friedman** "The Interrelationships of Self-Monitoring Factors, Personality Traits, and Nonverbal Social Skills. *Journal of Nonverbal Behavior, 7,* 1982, pp. 33–45.

——— and **H.S. Friedman** "Individual Differences and Cues to Deception." *Journal of Personality and Social Psychology, 45,* 1983, pp. 899–915.

——— and **H.S. Friedman** "Impression Formation: The Role of Expressive Behavior." *Journal of Personality and Social Psychology, 50,* 1986, pp. 421–27.

———— **H.S. Friedman** and **M.R. DiMatteo** "Nonverbal Greetings: Effects of the Situation and Personality." *Personality and Social Psychology Bulletin,* 7, 1981, pp. 682–89.

———— and **B. Throckmorton** "The Relative Effects of Verbal and Nonverbal Behavior, Appearance, and Social Skills on Evaluations Made in Hiring Interviews." *Journal of Applied Social Psychology,* in press.

———— and **J. Tucker.** "Verbal and Nonverbal Cues as Mediators of Ability to Deceive." Unpublished manuscript, 1987.

———— **J. Tucker** and **B. Throckmorton** "Social Skills and Deception Ability." *Personality and Social Psychology Bulletin,* in press.

Rosenman, R.H. et al. "Coronary Heart Disease in the Western Collaborative Group Study: Final Follow-up Experience of 8½ years." *Journal of the American Medical Association, 233,* 1975, pp. 872–77.

Rosenthal, R. (Ed.) *Skill in Nonverbal Communication: Individual Differences.* Cambridge, MA: Oelgeschlager, Gunn, & Hain, 1979.

———— et al. *Sensitivity to Nonverbal Communication: The PONS Test.* Baltimore, MD: Johns Hopkins University Press, 1979.

Rubenstein, C. and **P. Shaver** *In Search of Intimacy.* New York: Delacorte Press, 1982.

Salinger, J.D. *The Catcher in the Rye.* Boston, MA: Little, Brown, & Co., 1951.

Schiffer, I. *Charisma: A Psychoanalytic Look at Mass Society.* Toronto: University of Toronto Press, 1973.

Schlesinger, A.M., Jr. *A Thousand Days: John F. Kennedy in the White House.* New York: Fawcet Premier Books, 1965.

———— *Robert Kennedy and His Times.* Boston, MA: Houghton Mifflin, 1978.

Schneider, D.J., A.H. Hastorf and **P.C. Ellsworth** *Person Perception.* Reading, MA: Addison Wesley, 1979.

Schweitzer, A. "Theory and Political Charisma." *Comparative Studies in Society and History,* 1974, pp. 150–87.

Shumaker, S.A. and **A. Brownell** (Eds.). "Social Support." *Journal of Social Issues, Vols.* 40(4) and 41(1), 1984; 1985.

Snyder, M. "Self-Monitoring of Expressive Behavior." *Journal of Personality and Social Psychology, 30,* 1974, pp. 526–37.

——— "Self-Monitoring Processes." In L. Berkowitz (Ed.). *Advances in Experimental Social Psychology: 12.* New York: Academic Press, 1979.

——— *Public Appearances/Private Realities: The Psychology of Self-Monitoring.* New York: W.H. Freeman, 1987.

——— **E.D. Tanke** and **E. Berscheid** "Social Perception and Interpersonal Behavior: On the Self-fulfilling Nature of Social Stereotypes." *Journal of Personality and Social Psychology, 35,* 1977, pp. 656–66.

Sorenson, T.C. *Kennedy.* New York: Harper & Row, 1965.

Stein, G.H. (Ed.) *Hitler.* Englewood Cliffs, NJ: Prentice-Hall, 1968.

Thorndike, E.L. "Intelligence and Its Uses." *Harper's Magazine, 140,* 1920, pp. 227–35.

Thorndike, R.L. "Factor Analysis of Social and Abstract Intelligence." *Journal of Educational Psychology, 27,* 1936, pp. 231–33.

——— and **S. Stein** "An Evaluation of the Attempts to Measure Social Intelligence." *Psychological Bulletin, 34,* 1937, pp. 275–85.

Throckmorton, B. "Interrelationship of Communication Skills and Interviewing Success." Unpublished manuscript.

Toffler, A. *Future Shock.* New York: Random House, 1970.

Traupmann, J. and **E. Hatfield** "Love and Its Effect on Mental and Physical Health." In R. Fogel et al. (Eds.), *Aging: Stability and Change in the Family.* New York: Academic Press, 1981.

Twentyman, C.T. (Ed.) "Social Skills Training." *Behavioral Counseling Quarterly, 1,* 1981, pp. 225–319.

Vanderbilt, A. *Amy Vanderbilt's New Complete Book of Etiquette.* Garden City, NY: Doubleday & Co., 1963.

Walster, E. et al. "Importance of Physical Attractiveness in Dating Behavior." *Journal of Personality and Social Psychology,* 4, 1966, pp. 508–16.

Weber, M. *On Charisma and Institution Building.* Chicago: University of Chicago Press, 1968.

Wheeler-Bennett, J. *Action This Day: Working With Churchill.* London: MacMillan & Co., 1968.

White, T.H. *The Making of the President 1960.* New York: Atheneum, 1961.

——— *America in Search of Itself: The Making of the President 1956–1980.* New York: Harper & Row, 1982.

Wine, J.D. and **M.D. Smye** (Eds.) *Social Competence.* New York: Guilford, 1981.

Wolfgang, A. (Ed.) *Nonverbal Behavior: Perspectives, Applications, Intellectual Insights.* Lewiston, NY: Hogrefe, 1984.

Youngs, J.W.T. *Eleanor Roosevelt: A Personal and Public Life.* Boston, MA: Little, Brown, & Co., 1985.

Zimbardo, P. *Shyness,* Reading, MA: Addison-Wesley, 1977.

Index

W

Walster, William, 66
Weber, Max, 73–74
White, Theodore H., 107, 108

"White lies," 42–43
"Women's intuition," 47

Z

Zimbardo, Philip, Dr., 147, 148